CARIBBEAN COOKERY
SECRETS

CARIBBEAN COOKERY SECRETS

HOW TO COOK 100 OF THE MOST POPULAR WEST INDIAN, CAJUN AND CREOLE DISHES

David and Gwendolyn Daley

A HOW TO BOOK

ROBINSON

ROBINSON

First published in Great Britain in 2013 by Right Way,
an imprint of Constable and Robinson

This edition published in 2015 by Robinson

Copyright © David and Gwendolyn Daley 2013

3 5 7 9 10 8 6 4 2

The moral right of the authors has been asserted.

A CIP catalogue record for this book
is available from the British Library.

ISBN: 978-0-71602-298-5

Quotation from NHS Website @How to Prepare and Cook Food Safely'
www.nhs/Livewell/homehygine/Pages/Foodhygine.aspx
© Crown Copyright used in accordance with
the Open Government License for Public Sector Information
(see: www.nationalarchives.gov.uk/doc/open-government-licence)

Printed and bound in Great Britain by Clays Ltd, St Ives plc

Papers used by Robinson are from well-managed forests
and other responsible sources

MIX
Paper from
responsible sources
FSC® C104740

Robinson
An imprint of
Little, Brown Book Group
Carmelite House
50 Victoria Embankment
London EC4Y 0DZ

An Hachette UK Company
www.hachette.co.uk

www.littlebrown.co.uk

NOTE: The material contained in this book is set out in good faith for general guidance and no
liability can be accepted for loss or expense incurred as a result of relying in particular circumstances
on statements made in the book. Laws and regulations are complex and liable to change, and readers
should check the current position with relevant authorities before making personal arrangements.

How To Books are published by Robinson, an imprint of Little, Brown Book Group.
We welcome proposals from authors who have first-hand experience of their subjects. Please
set out the aims of your book, its target market and its suggested contents in an email
to Nikki.Read@howtobooks.co.uk

CONTENTS

INTRODUCTION

What is the secret of Caribbean/West Indian cooking?

Answer: **time** *and* **thyme**. *'Time' in terms of the fact that most Caribbean dishes must be marinated for several hours (or preferably overnight) prior to cooking; and 'thyme' because it's one of the most popular and common ingredients in Caribbean cooking.*

The food of the Caribbean is as diverse as its people and languages, drawing its cultural influences from Africa, Asia, Britain, France, India and Spain.

This book is not designed to cover every single technique, ingredient and cooking method used in Caribbean cooking, but rather to give you an overview of the most commonly used techniques, ingredients and cooking methods.

This book *will*:

- Show you the ingredients and common cooking methods used across all the islands of the Caribbean.
- Give you practical tips on how to make your Caribbean dish look and taste authentic.
- Give you practical advice on where to purchase all your essential Caribbean cooking utensils and ingredients, even if you live in a remote area.
- Correct the mistakes often seen on TV when celebrity chefs attempt to cook authentic Caribbean food.

It's important to realize that Caribbean cooking techniques, methods and ingredients not only vary from island to island, but also within communities, districts, parishes and also from family to family. While there is strictly no right or wrong way to cook a particular dish there are, however, certain techniques and generally accepted principles that will give you an authentically looking and tasting dish.

This book will take you on a journey across the Caribbean and introduce you to the most popular dishes cooked in: Anguilla, Antigua & Barbuda, Aruba, the Bahamas, Barbados, the British Virgin Islands, the Cayman Islands, Colombia, Cuba, Curaçao, Dominica, the Dominican Republic, Grenada, Guadeloupe, Haiti, Honduras, Jamaica, Martinique, Montserrat, Puerto Rico, St Barthélemy, St Kitts & Nevis, St Lucia, St Vincent & the Grenadines, Trinidad & Tobago, St Martin, and the United States Virgin Islands.
Enjoy!

David and Gwendolyn Daley

MEAT AND FISH PREPARATION – CARIBBEAN STYLE

In Caribbean culture it is a widely held practice to wash meat and fish in vinegar and/or lime juice prior to marinating and cooking. This practice dates back to times before pre-packaged supermarket foods and widely available refrigeration, where fresh meat and fish were killed and/or purchased daily, often with the entrails still inside. The acidic properties of vinegar or lime juice helped to kill bacteria and remove any unpleasant odours.

However, the washing of meat and fish is not something that is generally done in the UK. NHS guidelines on How to Prepare and Cook Food Safely state: 'Lots of people think they should wash raw chicken, but there's no need,' says food hygiene expert Adam Hardgrave. 'Any germs on it will be killed if you cook it thoroughly. In fact, if you do wash chicken, you could splash germs on to the sink, worktop, dishes or anything else nearby.'

Nevertheless, a widely reported study, undertaken by Good Housekeeping's microbiologist, Gina Marino, concluded that vinegar effectively kills 99.9 per cent of bacteria. Also, in a 2003 study at the University of Florida, researchers tested vinegar on food contaminated with E. coli and other germs. It found that a vinegar based mixture reduced bacteria by 90 per cent and viruses by about 95 per cent. (See: www.ncbi.nlm.nih.gov/pubmed/12597475.)

Whether or not you decide to wash your meat and fish in vinegar or lime juice in accordance with Caribbean traditions is a matter of personal preference.

It is, however, strongly advised that prior to marinating and cooking meat and fish you should as part of your meat preparation: (a) always inspect and smell meat or fish for freshness; (b) use a sharp knife to trim off any excess skin, fat or sinew; and (c) remove any damaged flesh or blood residue (clots) as they may spoil the flavour of your dish.

ESSENTIAL CARIBBEAN COOKING EQUIPMENT/ UTENSILS

A Dutch Pot (aka 'Dutchie')

This thick-walled cooking pot, usually made of cast aluminium, with a fitted lid, is used for the slow cooking of authentic Caribbean dishes. Dutch Pots come in both round and flat-bottomed varieties and can be used on top of a stove, in an oven, or, as per the traditional method, in a pit dug in the ground, heated by coals or hot rocks.

Both varieties of Dutch Pot are perfect for slowly cooking, stewing, frying or boiling a vast variety of authentic Caribbean dishes. In short, if you do not have a Dutch Pot you cannot call yourself an authentic Caribbean cook.

The two most common brands of Dutch Pot available today are the *Jamaica Sun* and *Guycan* brands. Dutch Pots are now available via the internet from *Amazon*, *eBay* and other online retailers, and start from around £20 (USD $30 or EU€25).

Secret: *Dutch Pots* are not to be confused with *Dutch Ovens* which, although very similar and can do roughly the same job, will not convince your friends and family that you are an authentic Caribbean cook.

A Tawa/Tava

This is a flat or concave disc-shaped griddle pan made from metal (cast aluminium, cast iron or steel) which is used for cooking a variety of flat breads (rotis, bakes, etc). Tawas originated in the Indian subcontinent, but are widely used throughout central, south and west Asia and beyond. Caribbean tawas are most commonly found in Trinidad and Guyana, but are used throughout the Caribbean. Once again, tawas are available online from a variety of retailers.

ESSENTIAL CARIBBEAN COOKING INGREDIENTS AND TERMS

Ackee
A fruit which originally came from West Africa, but has become a Jamaican favourite, ackee is one of the main ingredients in the Jamaican national dish of *Ackee and Salt Fish*. The flesh of ackee has a soft, creamy yellow flesh, which is often said to have a scrambled-egg-like texture. Ackee is a fruit that grows on trees, and can only be eaten when it is ripe, and the skin of the fruit has changed from green to a bright yellowy-red. In the UK and US ackee is only available in tins/cans as it needs to be specially harvested in order to ensure that it is safe to eat. Leading Jamaican brands for the canned variety include: *Dunn's River, Grace, Hi-Lo, Jamaica Sun, Juliana, Island Sun* and *Linstead Market*.

All Purpose Seasoning (Caribbean Dried Seasonings)
There is a wide variety of Caribbean all purpose seasonings (with specific varieties for meat, poultry and fish) available on the market. These seasonings can be used to marinate meat or fish prior to cooking. Most varieties contain a high level of salt so should be used very conservatively. In most recipes in this book where all purpose or other seasonings have been listed, we have intentionally deleted salt from the ingredients list.

Allspice
See: *Pimenta Berry*.

Ambarella
See: *Golden Apple*.

Bananas (Green Banana, Green Figs, Sweet Bananas)
Green banana (commonly known as green fig) is the unripe, green, version of the common yellow, sweet bananas we all know and love. In Caribbean cooking green bananas/green figs form one of the 'Ground

Provisions'/'Hard Food' which are boiled or roasted and used as a substitute for rice. Sweet bananas are the commonly available, yellow, ripe version of the green banana.

Bammy (Bami)
A traditional Caribbean flatbread made from grated cassava and flour which is fried and served for breakfast.

Black-Eyed Peas (Black-Eyed Beans, California Black-Eye Peas)
An edible light brown bean with a black 'eye' in the centre, which is used (hot or cold) in Caribbean rice and salad dishes (see: Rice & Peas, page 22). Available dried or canned.

Breadfruit
A very large, green fruit that grows on a breadfruit tree with a green skin and a creamy white flesh which tastes a bit like bread. Breadfruit is usually roasted, then, once it has cooled, is cut into segments and fried.

Callaloo (Callaloo Bush)
A Caribbean green leaf vegetable similar to spinach (but with larger leaves and thicker shoots) which is puréed to make soup (Cream of Callaloo Soup) or steamed with salt fish and onions (Salt Fish and Callaloo). Fresh callaloo can be found in your local ethnic food store or market, but is also available in 540 g and 285 g tins/cans with brands such as *Dunn's River, Grace, Island Sun* and *Jamaica Sun*.

Chadon Beni (Chadon, Shadon, Shado Beni or Shadow Benny, Bandhania, Culantro or Thai Parsley)
One of the key ingredients in authentic Trinidadian cooking and, in particular, Trinidadian Green Seasoning. Chadon Beni is a herb which can often be found in the larger Oriental supermarkets if you ask for 'Thai Parsley'. If you are unable to find a ready supply of Chadon Beni you can use fresh coriander (known as cilantro in the US) as a substitute.

Chocho/Cho-cho (Chayote, Christophene, Christophine, Mirliton, Merleton, Pear Squash, Vegetable Pear)
Mild-flavoured squash which looks like a large, wrinkled, pale green pear and is known by many different names. Used in Caribbean cooking in soups or boiled and served with other vegetables.

Christophene or Christophine
See: *Chocho.*

Culantro
See: *Chadon Beni.*

Dasheen (Taro, Eddo or Malanga)
The edible starchy yellow tubers (corms or cormels) of the taro plant. In Caribbean cooking dasheen corms/cormels are peeled, chopped and then used as a root vegetable in the cooking of Saturday Soups (see: Recipe Nos. 35 or 39) or boiled with other Ground Provisions (see: Recipe No. 65) and served as an accompaniment to other meat and fish dishes. Dasheen can also be dried and then ground down to make flour.

Escallion (Scallion, Green Onion)
One of the fundamental plants that has helped to give Jamaican cuisine its distinctive flavour. Escallions are also known by some people as *green onions* or *onion sticks.* Though closely related to onions, escallion does have a milder flavour (and a smaller bulb). It is very rare to find genuine escallion plants to buy in any shops or markets in the UK or USA, but you can use 'spring onions' as a viable substitute. Genuine escallion plants are grown in Jamaica and Trinidad & Tobago (where it is known as 'chive'). Fresh escallion is difficult to find and expensive outside Jamaica and Trinidad, but dried Caribbean spice mixtures that include escallion are widely available.
    Secret: How do you know if you have come across a genuine escallion plant? *The bulbs of a genuine escallion plant have a distinctive purple and white colouring, with a green stem/stake.* (For images see: http://foodguidejamaica.com/local-crops.)

Escovitch
A style of Jamaican cooking using vinegar, onions, peppers and spices, used predominantly for fish dishes (see: Recipe No. 24, Escovitch Fish).

Golden Apple (June Plum or Ambarella)
This fruit is widely available on most Caribbean islands and in Asia, but is more difficult to find in other areas of the world. The fruits, which are borne in clusters at the tips of branches, have a thin skin that is green and shiny, which changes to golden yellow upon ripening.

Green Fig/Green Banana

The unripe version of the conventional yellow banana, which forms one of the 'Ground Provisions' ('Hard Food') of Caribbean cooking. Not to be confused with plantain. The main way to tell the difference between green fig/green banana and plantain is that the latter tends to be large with a thicker skin.

Green Pigeon Peas (Cajanus Cajan – aka Gandule Verdes Tropical Green Peas, Green Gungo Peas, Congo Peas)

An edible green pea/bean that is used (hot or cold) in Caribbean rice and salad dishes (see: Pigeon Peas & Rice, page 44). Available dried or canned.

Green Seasoning

The key ingredient of authentic Trinidad & Tobago cooking. Green Seasoning is a blend of herbs and spices which is used in stews and other meat dishes to give Trinidadian cooking its unique flavour.

Ground Provisions (Hard Food)

A term used in Caribbean cooking to collectively describe root and other vegetables such as breadfruit, cassava, chocho, dasheen, green banana (green fig), plantain, sweet potatoes and yams.

Fig

See: *Green Fig/Green Banana*.
Not to be confused with the *common fig* fruit of the Mediterranean and Middle East.

Hard Food

See: *Ground Provisions*.

Jerk

A method of slow cooking meat and fish, using the marinade of the same name (Jerk Sauce/Jerk Seasoning), whose primary ingredients are the pimenta (allspice) berry and Scotch bonnet peppers. In Jamaica, authentic Jerk meats and fish are smoked/cooked slowly on a pimenta (also known as pimento) wood barbecue.

June Plum

See: *Golden Apple*.

Marjoram (Sweet Marjoram, Knotted Marjoram, Sweet Oregano)
A perennial, cold-sensitive herb with sweet pine and citrus flavour that originates from the Mediterranean and is used in Caribbean cooking (particularly in Barbados). Marjoram is called oregano in the USA. 'European Oregano' has a much stronger flavour than Marjoram, and is sometimes called '*Wild Marjoram*' outside of Europe.

Pimenta/Pimento Berry – (Allspice, *Pimenta Dioica*)
The dried, unripe berries from the pimenta tree are used extensively in Caribbean cooking and give curries and other savoury dishes that distinctive flavour. When dry it looks like a peppercorn but with a reddish brown colour. It is said that it tastes like a combination between cinnamon, cloves and nutmeg and this is the reason why it is called 'allspice'. In its ground form it is one of the key ingredients of Jerk (chicken, pork, fish) cooking. Also known as 'pimento', it should not be confused with pimento peppers.

Plantain
Plantains are a starchy, unsweetened variety of banana (called plantain banana in the USA) that are inedible raw and must be cooked (fried, roasted or boiled) before eating. Most are larger and slightly more angular in shape than 'sweet' bananas. Not to be confused with green fig/green banana or the common 'sweet' banana. The main way to tell the difference between green fig/green banana and plantain is that the latter tends to be large with a thicker skin. Colours vary depending on ripeness.

Salted Fish (Salt Fish, Saltfish)
Salted fish is fresh fish (cod, pollock or ling) that has been salt-cured and dried until all the moisture has been extracted. It needs to be rehydrated and most of the salt removed through a process of overnight soaking in hot water and subsequent boiling. The aim is *never to remove all* of the salt; enough salt should remain to taste. If it doesn't, you can end up with a bland piece of fish.
　　Warning: When buying dried salted fish it is suggested that you buy the *boneless and skinless* variety, as this cuts down on preparation time. However, salted fish is also now available in canned form, which although more expensive does not require rehydration. Leading brands of pre-packaged salted fish products available in the UK include: *Blue*

Ocean, Cawoods, Colombos, Grace, Island Sun and *Luscocod*. Products are usually available in 200 g, 300 g and 400 g packets.

Scotch Bonnet/Chilli Pepper (Boabs, Bonnet, Scotty Bons, Bonney Peppers, or Caribbean Red Peppers)
A variety of chilli pepper used widely in Caribbean cooking.

Warning: As with all chilli peppers, we recommend that you wear disposable rubber gloves when handling them to protect your skin from painful stings.

Sorrel (Roselle – plant)
The red sepals of the roselle plant which are dried and used in Caribbean cooking to make drinks and teas.

Soursop/Sour Sop (Guanabana, Custard Apple, Cherimoya or Sitaphal)
A large, green, prickly fruit of the soursop tree, which is found widely in the Caribbean, Central and South America. Its flesh has been described as a cottony white pulp, and its taste as a cross between pineapple and strawberry. Soursop is used to make drinks and punches (Recipe No. 98).

Thai Parsley
See: *Chadon Beni*.

Yams
There are many different varieties of yams, including yellow yam, white yam, (St) Lucian yam, Renta (Barbados) yam, sweet yam, soft yams, Yampi (African) yam, and taw yam. Yams are one of the key 'Ground Provisions' or 'Hard Food' which form a staple part of the Caribbean diet. Yams can be served with most meat and fish dishes and together with other 'Ground Provisions' are used as a substitute for rice. Yams can be baked, boiled, fried, grilled, smoked or roasted and are therefore a very versatile vegetable.

MEASUREMENTS
IN THE RECIPES

The American cup measurement is widely used in the Caribbean and is therefore used in our recipes.

For liquids

1 cup	240 ml	8 fl oz
½ cup	120 ml	4 fl oz

For dry ingredients

The exact measurement depends on the ingredient involved, but the following is a rough guide.

1 cup flour	150 g	5 oz
1 cup caster/granulated sugar	225 g	8 oz
1 cup brown sugar	175 g	6 oz
1 cup butter/margarine	225 g	8 oz
1 cup currants	150 g	5 oz
1 cup ground almonds	110 g	4 oz
1 cup uncooked rice	200 g	7 oz
1 cup grated cheese	110 g	4 oz

Although we generally give the metric and imperial equivalents in the recipes as well as the cup measurements, it's easier if you use the cup measurements so we recommend you purchase a set of American cup measures which can be purchased from many outlets on the internet.

THE RECIPES

No. 1 JERK CHICKEN

Most likely to be found in: Jamaica.

THE SECRET: Authentic Jerk Chicken is made with a combination of three things: (a) The Jerk Dry Rub (a dry pre-seasoning which penetrates the meat); (b) Jerk Marinade (a wet marinade, which is used for pre-seasoning and as a basting sauce to keep the meat moist and succulent during cooking); and (c) a Jerk Dipping Sauce (optional), which is sometimes poured over the meat after cooking. In Jamaica, authentic Jerk meats and fish are smoked/cooked slowly on a pimenta (also known as pimento) wood barbecue.

OTHER BACKGROUND INFORMATION:
- Jerk meats (or fish) should be cooked slowly on a low heat barbecue (when the coals are white) or grilled, with meat (or fish) being turned frequently and basted in Jerk Marinade in order to maintain moisture.
- Allspice (pimenta/pimento berry) is the key ingredient for genuine authenticity, and is now widely available, in seed or ground form.
- Genuine Jerk meats (or fish) are barbecued/smoked with pimenta leaves or pimenta wood (not widely available) being added to the barbecue coals, which also adds to the authentic taste. Oak wood chips can be used as a substitute for pimenta leaves or wood.
- Pimenta wood is not widely available outside Jamaica, but can be mail ordered via the internet as charcoal, wood chips or planks from a US company called Exotic Wood Chips LLC, via the following website: www.pimentowood.com.

INGREDIENTS (SERVES 6):

6 portions of chicken quarters (legs and thighs)
3 tsp vinegar/lime juice (optional)
3 tsp Jerk Rub (see: Recipe No. 51)
2 tsp oil
3 tsp Jerk Marinade (see: Recipe No. 52)
1 portion (50 ml/2 fl oz) of Jerk Dipping Sauce
   (see: Recipe No. 53)

METHOD:

1. Prepare the chicken using the vinegar/lime juice (optional). (See: *Meat and Fish Preparation – Caribbean Style*, page 9.)
2. Remove the excess liquid.
3. With a sharp knife trim off any excess fat, skin or sinew.
4. Place the chicken portions in a bowl. Add the Jerk Rub, oil and stir.
5. Leave the chicken to marinate in the refrigerator for at least 4 hours, preferably overnight.
6. Grill on a barbecue (or using an oven's grill setting) on medium heat (the barbecue coals should be white) for 25–30 minutes.
7. Turn the chicken regularly and baste in the Jerk Marinade.
8. The chicken is cooked when there is no pink meat and the juices run clear and are no longer pink or red.
9. **Optional step:** Using a cleaver and chopping board, chop each chicken quarter into several smaller pieces (through the bones and joints). **NB:** Use a kitchen fork to keep the chicken in place.
10. **Tip:** Use a food thermometer to check the core temperature of cooked chicken (74°C/165°F).
11. Serve with rice and peas, salad and Jerk Dipping Sauce.

No. 2 RICE & PEAS

Most likely to be found in: Jamaica and all over the Caribbean.
Alternative Names: Peas & Rice, Beans & Rice, Rice & Beans.

THE SECRET: A few tips:

1. If using tinned/canned beans/peas DO NOT drain off the dark brown/red salted water that comes with the beans/peas, as this helps to give the rice grains colour. It sounds obvious to those in the know, but when cooked the rice grains in your rice and peas should be a lighter shade of the beans/peas used (i.e. a light brown, beige or light red).
2. The rice should be one of the last ingredients added to the cooking process, as this will prevent the rice from overcooking.
3. If your rice lacks colour, replace the salt with dark soya sauce or gravy browning. Try not to add too much water.
4. If you really want to impress, DO NOT use kidney beans (*red peas*) which are widely available, but instead try *black-eye peas, brown gungo peas* (aka *brown pigeon peas*) or one of the many varieties of *cowpea* which have much more interesting flavours.
5. Finally, if you have the time the most authentic method is to use dried peas/beans which are soaked overnight and then cooked before adding other ingredients.

OTHER BACKGROUND INFORMATION: Having watched many television programmes where 'celebrity chefs' have attempted to cook authentic rice and peas, it is amazing how often they get the colour of the dish wrong.

INGREDIENTS (SERVES 6–8):

1 tbsp vegetable oil
3 escallions or spring onions, diced
3 cloves of garlic, crushed or finely chopped
1 x 400 g tin/can dark red beans (black-eyed peas, brown gungo (pigeon) peas or red kidney beans – including the liquid for colour)
2 cups/480 ml/16 fl oz water
1 x 400 ml tin/can coconut milk
3 sprigs of fresh thyme or 3 tsp dried thyme
1 tsp salt (to taste) or 2 tsp dark soya sauce/gravy browning
1 tsp black pepper
2 cups/400 g/14 oz long grain or basmati rice (The ratio of cooked to uncooked rice is approximately 3:1.)
1 uncut Scotch bonnet or jalapeno pepper (optional)

METHOD:

1. Heat the oil in your Dutch Pot/heavy-bottomed pan (with lid).
2. Add the diced escallions or spring onions to the pan/pot.
3. Sauté for 2 minutes and then add the garlic.
4. Add the peas/beans, water, coconut milk, thyme and other seasoning and bring to the boil.
5. Check the colour of the liquid/broth, which should be a light brown/beige colour.
6. Taste the liquid/broth and correct the seasoning.
7. **Tip:** Add soya sauce/gravy browning for colour if the liquid/broth is too light.
8. Add the rice and the whole Scotch bonnet (if using), then stir. The level of the broth/water should cover the rice by about 1 inch.
9. Bring all the ingredients to the boil.
10. Reduce the heat to the lowest temperature and then cover with the lid or silver foil over the top of your pan/Dutch Pot.
11. Cook the rice for 35–45 minutes adding more water if necessary, but not too much otherwise the rice will go mushy.
12. Use a fork to test if the rice is cooked (this prevents the rice grains breaking).
13. Serve with Jerk Chicken or other meat or fish dishes.

No. 3 PEPPERPOT

(NATIONAL DISH: GUYANA)

Most likely to be found in: Guyana, Jamaica, Trinidad & Tobago,
plus other Caribbean Islands.
Alternative Names: Guyana Pepperpot, Pepperpot Stew.

THE SECRET: Cassareep (aka *Cassarep Pomeroon* – a preservative,
made from the juice of the bitter, grated cassava root, flavoured with
cinnamon and brown sugar). The most popular brand of *Cassareep*
available in the UK is called *Cassava Sauce*. There is also a brand called
Brown Betty Pomeroon Cassareep which is available in the US.

OTHER BACKGROUND INFORMATION: Guyanese Pepperpot is
an Amerindian dish, which was traditionally served at special events such
as Christmas. There are several different variations of this dish cooked
around the Caribbean. The Guyanese version is deemed to be the most
authentic as it is the only version that contains Cassareep. Authentic
Pepperpot also uses ingredients like chopped *tripe* and *cowfoot*, instead of
stewing steak. You can also substitute bacon for the pickled pig tails if
you wish. Generally the dish is made in a large pot and can be kept in
the refrigerator for several days, reheated before eating.

INGREDIENTS (SERVES 6):
450 g/1 lb pickled pig tails or salt beef
3 tbsp lime juice (optional)
900 g/2 lb stewing steak
450 g/1 lb oxtail
1 cup cassareep
1 x 2.5 cm/1 inch piece dried orange or lemon peel
6 sprigs of fresh thyme
1 x 2.5 cm/1 inch piece stick cinnamon
3 heads of clove
50 g/2 oz sugar
1 or 2 hot peppers
salt (to taste)

METHOD:
1. Pre-soak the pickled pig tails/salt beef overnight to remove the salt.
2. Prepare the meats using the lime juice (optional). (See: *Meat and Fish Preparation – Caribbean Style*, page 9.)
3. Remove the excess liquid.
4. With a sharp knife trim off any excess fat or sinew.
5. Put the pig tails (or salt beef) in a heavy pan. Cover with water and bring to the boil. Skim.
6. When half-tender, add the other meats, and hot water to cover. Cook for about one hour. Cut all the meats into 0.5 cm/¼ inch pieces.
7. Add the other ingredients and simmer until the meat is tender. Adjust the flavour by adding a little salt and sugar.
8. Serve hot.

NB: Due to the preservative properties of cassareep, this dish can be kept for several days. Refrigerate after use and reheat to 75°C before eating.

No. 4 JAMAICAN PATTIES

Most likely to be found in: Jamaica.
Alternative Names: Patty, Patties.

THE SECRET: The secret of a good patty is in the filling and the pastry. This sounds obvious, but a good pastry is made by: (a) the minimum handling of the dough before baking; (b) keeping all the pastry ingredients and utensils cold (including your hands); and (c) adding the liquid a little at a time. With regard to the filling use quality ingredients such as quality minced meat with no fat or gristle.

OTHER BACKGROUND INFORMATION: However, you decide to eat your patty, don't forget the ginger beer!

To make a vegetarian filling for the patties used diced potato, peas, corn, carrots and cabbage. You can also experiment with several different fillings including chicken (curry or Jerk), salt fish, fish and seafood.

INGREDIENTS (SERVES 8–10):
Filling (Meat):
900 g/2 lb lean stewing beef, cut into small pieces/ground minced/ground beef
1 large onion, chopped
1 tbsp Jamaican curry powder
2 sprigs of thyme, finely chopped
1 Scotch bonnet pepper, chopped and deseeded
1 tsp salt
2 escallion/green onion stalks, chopped
½ cup/120 ml/4 fl oz beef stock
1½ cups breadcrumbs

Pastry:
900 g/2 lb plain/all-purpose flour
1 tbsp ground turmeric
1 cup grated suet/shortening
250 g/9 oz cold margarine
560 ml/1 pint ice-cold water (refrigerated)

METHOD:
Make Pastry:
1. In a large bowl mix the flour, turmeric, suet, and margarine together until they look like crumbs.
2. Add the cold water to the mixture to make dough.
3. Sprinkle some flour on your cleaned work surface and roll the dough with a rolling pin.
4. Roll until the dough is about 3 mm/⅛ inch thick.
5. Cut round a saucer or bowl to make circles in the dough.
6. Let the pieces sit in a bowl for about 30 minutes, or while you are making the meat filling.

Make Filling:
1. If using stewing beef prepare the meat by trimming off any excess fat or skin with a sharp knife.
2. Brown the beef/mince in a frying pan, and then add the onion, curry powder, thyme, Scotch bonnet pepper, salt, and escallion.
3. Turn the heat to medium.
4. Fold in the ingredients with a wooden spoon.
5. Add the beef stock and allow the meat to cook for about 20 minutes.
6. Fold in the breadcrumbs.
7. Cook for another 7 minutes, taste the meat and add more salt if needed.

Baking:
1. Pre-heat the oven to 350°F/180°C/Gas Mark 4.
2. Add spoons of meat filling to the pre-cut dough pieces.
3. Fold over the dough to form a half-moon shape.
4. Use the end of a dining fork to seal the crescent edge of the patty while making a pattern.
5. Place the patties on a lightly greased baking sheet.
6. Brush the top of each patty with egg or milk.
7. Bake for about 30–35 minutes.

No. 5 STEW CHICKEN

(TRINIDADIAN METHOD)

Most likely to be found in: Trinidad & Tobago, Jamaica and other Caribbean Islands (but with slightly different cooking methods and ingredients).
Alternative Name: Brown Stew Chicken.

THE SECRET: Do not burn the sugar, as this will give the dish a burnt aftertaste. Mastering how to brown meat using caramelized sugar takes a bit of practice, but once you have done so you will get your friends and family talking.

The use of a quality Green Seasoning will give this dish its authentic taste.

OTHER BACKGROUND INFORMATION: Green Seasoning is a blend of puréed Chadon Beni, garlic, thyme, salt, pepper, hot pepper (Scotch bonnet) and vegetable (olive) oil, which is used to season meat and fish in Trinidad & Tobago.

Green Seasoning is now widely available in ethnic food stores and on the internet. Leading brands include *Baron, Caribbean Crescent, Chef Condiments* and *Marbel's.* However, if you really want to be adventurous you can try and make your own (see: Recipe No. 59).

INGREDIENTS (SERVES 6):

1 whole chicken, cut into 12 pieces/portions
1 tbsp white vinegar (optional)
2 limes, squeezed, or 2 tbsp lime juice (optional)
1 cup/240 ml/8 fl oz water (optional)
4 tbsp Green Seasoning
2 cloves of garlic, chopped
1 onion, chopped
salt and pepper
2 tbsp vegetable oil
1 tbsp brown sugar
1 cup/240 ml/8 fl oz chicken stock/broth
1–2 tsp pepper sauce (optional)

METHOD:

1. Prepare the chicken using the vinegar and/or lime juice and water (optional). (See: *Meat and Fish Preparation – Caribbean Style*, page 9.)
2. Remove the excess liquid.
3. With a sharp knife trim off any excess fat or sinew.
4. Season the chicken with the Green Seasoning, garlic, onion, salt and pepper.
5. Leave the chicken to marinade for a minimum of 4 hours (or preferably overnight).
6. Heat the oil on high heat in your Dutch Pot/heavy-bottomed pan (with lid).
7. Add the sugar and allow to caramelize (golden brown bubbles should appear on top of the oil. Do not let it burn!).
8. Remove excess seasoning from the chicken, and set aside.
9. Add the chicken pieces, turning continuously, and allow to brown.
10. Add the remaining seasoning (from Step 8), along with the stock and the hot pepper sauce.
11. Reduce the heat and cook until the chicken is tender (but *not* falling off the bone).
12. Skim off excess oil from the top of the dish.
13. Serve with rice, vegetables and salad.

No. 6 BROWN STEW CHICKEN

(JAMAICAN STYLE)

Most likely to be found in: Jamaica.
Alternative Name: Stew Chicken.

THE SECRET: Brown Stew is simply a meat/fish dish in gravy. This is one dish where there is no standard colour. Gravy colours vary from a light beige, to a bright red or a deep dark brown. Much depends on the colour of the tomatoes used and whether gravy browning is added to dish.

OTHER BACKGROUND INFORMATION: 'Brown Stew' meats (chicken or beef) and fish are very popular in Jamaica largely due to the love of spicy gravies.

INGREDIENTS (SERVES 6):

1 whole chicken, cut into 12 pieces
2 tsp white vinegar (optional)
1 lime, squeezed, or 2 tsp lime juice (optional)
2 medium onions, chopped
3 medium tomatoes, chopped
4 escallion stalks, chopped
2 cloves of garlic, finely diced
1 hot (Scotch bonnet) pepper, without seeds, chopped
4 sprigs of fresh thyme or 2 tsp dried thyme
1 tsp ground pimenta (allspice)
2 tbsp soy sauce
1 tbsp vegetable oil
2 medium carrots, diced
2 tsp cornflour (cornstarch) (to thicken gravy)
1 x 400 ml tin/can coconut milk

METHOD:

1. Prepare the chicken using the vinegar/lime juice (optional). (See: *Meat and Fish Preparation – Caribbean Style*, page 9.)
2. Remove the excess liquid.
3. With a sharp knife trim off any excess fat, skin or sinew.
4. Add the onion, tomato, escallion, garlic, pepper, thyme, pimenta and soy sauce into a large bowl and marinade the chicken pieces.
5. Cover the chicken and leave to marinate for at least one hour (preferably overnight).
6. Heat the oil in a Dutch Pot or large frying pan.
7. Shake off the seasonings as you remove each piece of chicken from the marinade.
8. Reserve the marinade for the sauce.
9. Lightly brown the chicken a few pieces at a time in very hot oil.
10. Place the browned chicken pieces on a plate to rest while you brown the remaining pieces.
11. Drain off excess oil and return the chicken to the pan.
12. Pour the marinade over the chicken and add the carrot.
13. Stir and cook over medium heat for 10 minutes.
14. Mix the flour and coconut milk and add to the stew, stirring constantly.
15. Turn the heat down to minimum and cook for another 20 minutes or until tender.
16. Serve with Rice and Peas (Recipe No. 2) or plain rice and Fried Plantain (Recipe No. 23).

No. 7 CURRY GOAT

(JAMAICAN STYLE)

Most likely to be found in: Jamaica, and most other Caribbean islands.
Alternative Names: Curry Mutton; Curried Goat or Curried Mutton.

THE SECRET: It is tempting to add more curry power than the recipe suggests, but by doing this you may lose the unique flavour of the goat meat. The meat in Caribbean curries is marinated in the curry spices for several hours (or overnight) and then slow cooked for a deep, rice curry flavour.

OTHER BACKGROUND INFORMATION: On some Caribbean Islands people use the term 'Curry Goat' interchangeably with 'Curry Mutton'. Mutton comes from an adult sheep whereas goat meat comes from a goat! To the untrained eye it is easy to get confused but here are a few things to look out for. Goat meat (a) tends to have a gamier flavour than mutton; (b) is leaner and bonier than mutton; (c) when diced, goat meat tends to have more bones and less flesh than the equivalent weight of mutton.

INGREDIENTS (SERVES 6):
1.8 kg/4 lb goat meat/mutton, diced
1 fresh lime, squeezed, or 2 tsp lime juice (optional)
1 large onion, diced
1 bulb of garlic (approximately 6 cloves), finely diced
2 tsp salt
2 tsp black pepper
3 sprigs of fresh thyme or 1 tbsp dried thyme
2 whole Scotch bonnet peppers or 1–2 tsp pepper sauce
2 tbsp vegetable oil
3 escallion/green onion sprigs, chopped
3 tsp Jamaican curry powder
1 cup/240 ml/8 fl oz water (optional)
2 peeled potatoes, cut into cubes (optional)

METHOD:

1. Prepare the meat using the lime juice (optional). (See: *Meat and Fish Preparation – Caribbean Style*, page 9.)
2. Drain off the excess liquid.
3. With a sharp knife trim off any excess fat, skin or sinew.
4. Place the goat meat in a sealable container and add the onion, garlic, salt, black pepper, thyme, and Scotch bonnet pepper.
5. Wearing rubber gloves, rub the spices into the goat with your hands. Marinate, covered and refrigerated, for 4–6 hours (or preferably overnight).
6. In a large heavy pot, heat the oil over medium heat.
7. Add the goat with the marinade, escallion and curry powder. Stir thoroughly.
8. Cover the pot, reduce the heat to low, and simmer the goat slowly *in its own juices*, stirring occasionally, until the goat is nearly tender, about 30 minutes.
9. If the meat is tough, pour ½ cup of water at a time down the sides of the pot, not directly onto the goat (or you will toughen the meat).
10. When the meat is tender add the potatoes, if using.
11. Cover and simmer for 15 minutes or until the potatoes are cooked but not too soft.
12. If there is not enough curry sauce, add ½ cup water and simmer for another 5–10 minutes.
13. Serve with plain rice (or roti) and Fried Plantain.

No. 8 CHICKEN PELAU

Most likely to be found in: Trinidad & Tobago and Guyana.
Alternative Name: Chicken Pilau.

THE SECRET: Use a fork to stir and to check whether the rice is cooked in order to avoid breaking the grains during cooking. Rice and chicken should be dark brown in colour, but not taste burnt.

OTHER BACKGROUND INFORMATION: This dish can also be baked in the oven. The layer of caramelized rice at the very bottom of the pot is often called 'bun-bun' ('burn burn'). While this may be discarded by some, for many Caribbean natives this is their favourite part of the dish.

★This recipe can also be adapted into the vegetarian dish, **Vegetable Pilau** by replacing the chicken with diced potatoes, butternut squash, pumpkin, chopped okra, sweetcorn, green peas and diced carrots.

INGREDIENTS (SERVES 8–10):
900 g–1.3 kg/2–3 lb chicken pieces★ (legs or thighs)
3 tbsp of vinegar and/or 2 limes (optional)
2 tbsp Green Seasoning (see: Recipe No. 59)
1 medium onion, diced
½ tsp black pepper
3 cloves of garlic, crushed
1 tbsp tomato ketchup
2 tbsp Worcestershire sauce
2 tbsp soya sauce
3 tbsp oil
2 tbsp brown sugar
2 cups/400 g/14 oz long grain rice
1 x 400 g tin/can brown gungo, black-eyed or pigeon peas
1 x 400 g tin/can chick peas
1 Scotch bonnet/hot pepper (optional)
2 medium sized carrots, diced
1 x 400 ml tin/can/2 cups coconut milk
2 cups/480 ml/16 fl oz water
1 tbsp butter/margarine

METHOD:

1. Prepare the chicken using vinegar and/or lime juice (optional). (See: *Meat and Fish Preparation – Caribbean Style*, page 9.)
2. Remove the excess liquid.
3. With a sharp knife trim off any excess fat or sinew.
4. Season the chicken with the Green Seasoning, onion, pepper, garlic, tomato ketchup, Worcester sauce and soy sauce.
5. Leave to marinate for at least 4 hours or preferably overnight.
6. Heat the oil in a Dutch Pot on high heat.
7. Add the sugar to the pot, so that it is covered by oil, and allow to caramelize (until dark brown), but *not* to burn (blacken).
8. Carefully add the chicken pieces to the pot and stir frequently for 4–6 minutes until the pieces are browned.
9. Add the rice and stir for a further 3 minutes until the rice grains are browned.
10. Add the brown peas, chick peas, pepper and carrots, then stir into the mix.
11. Add the coconut milk, water, salt and pepper and a knob of butter then bring to the boil. NB At this stage the liquid should cover all the ingredients in the pot.
12. Lower the heat and cover the pot with foil and replace the lid.
13. Simmer for 30–40 minutes until the rice is cooked and all the liquid has evaporated.
14. If necessary, add additional hot water (1 tbsp at a time, every 5 minutes) if the rice is not cooked.

No. 9 PARATHA ROTI

(SKIN ONLY)

Most likely to be found in: Trinidad, Guyana
and other islands in the Caribbean.
Alternative Name: Buss-up-shot.

THE SECRET: Authentic Caribbean rotis should be very light, soft and moist. This is achieved by using a very fine flour and working the dough correctly. Perfection will not be achieved easily and may take years of practice.

OTHER BACKGROUND INFORMATION: In the Caribbean a plain, refined flour is used to make roti skins. This differs from the heavier atta flour used in the Indian sub-continent. Other varieties of roti skin include: Dahl Puri roti (roti skin filled with a mixture of finely ground split peas, cumin (jeera, often known as 'geera' in the Caribbean) and garlic); Aloo Puri roti (roti skin filled with a mixture of finely ground potatoes, cumin and garlic).

INGREDIENTS (SERVES 6):
450 g/1 lb/4 cups flour
4 tsp baking powder
1 tsp salt
1½ cups/360 ml/12 fl oz water (approx)
30 g/1½ oz/3 tbsp soft ghee, suet or butter (soft – at room temperature)
120 ml/4 fl oz/½ cup oil (for cooking)

EQUIPMENT:
tawa/tava or non-stick frying pan
wooden spatula
pastry brush
rolling pin

METHOD:
1. Sieve the flour, baking powder and salt into a bowl.
2. Mix in enough water to create a soft, smooth dough.
3. Knead the dough well. Cover with a damp cloth and leave to relax for approximately 1½ hours.
4. Once the dough is relaxed, re-knead and divide into 4 balls (aka 'loyahs').
5. Leave the balls/loyahs to rest for about 20–30 minutes.
6. Sprinkle a small amount of flour onto a smooth surface and roll out the dough balls into a thin circle of approximately 22.5 cm/9 inches in diameter.
7. Add ghee (or butter) and oil to a bowl and use a wooden spoon to mix a smooth oily liquid.
8. Spread the soft ghee mixture, suet or butter over the surface of the rolled dough, and sprinkle with flour.
9. Make a cut from the centre out to the edge and roll up the dough into a cone.
10. Press the peak and flatten the centre of the dough cone.
11. Leave to 'rest' for a further 20–30 minutes.
12. Once rested, roll out the dough (roti skin) again on a floured surface into thin circles of approximately 22.5 cm/9 inches in diameter.
13. Using the flat side of a cup or other utensil, dip into the melted butter or ghee and coat an already hot tava.
14. Place the dough onto the tava to cook.
15. Spread the ghee mixture (or butter on one side of the roti skin using the flat edge of the cup.
16. Then turn the roti skin onto the other side and repeat the process.
17. Once the roti skin is cooked on both sides, it can be placed in a clean tea towel, crushed and then ripped.
18. Serve with curried meat, potatoes and other vegetables.

No. 10 STEWED OXTAIL & BUTTER BEANS

Most likely to be found: All over the Caribbean.
Alternative Names: Oxtail Stew, Oxtail.

THE SECRET: Oxtail must be cooked slowly in order to ensure a tender palatable dish. The authentic dish has a deep brown colour, which can be achieved by adding additional dark soy sauce or gravy browning

OTHER BACKGROUND INFORMATION: If you wish to speed up the cooking process you can use a pressure cooker.

Tip: Ask your butcher to trim off excess fat from oxtail, as this will reduce cooking/rendering time.

INGREDIENTS (SERVES 6):
900 g–1.3 kg/2–3 lb chopped oxtail pieces, trimmed
3 tbsp vinegar (optional)
2 escallions, finely chopped
½ Scotch bonnet pepper or other variety of hot pepper
1 tbsp chopped/grated ginger
4 cloves of garlic, crushed
4 sprigs of fresh thyme
½ tsp allspice (ground pimenta)
2 tbsp dark soy sauce
salt and black pepper (to taste)
1 tbsp oil for cooking
5 cups/1.2 litres/2 pints water (enough to cover the meat)
1 medium size onion, chopped
225 g/½ lb carrots
1 x 400 g tin/can butter beans (lima beans – drained)

METHOD:

1. Prepare the oxtail using the vinegar (optional). (See: *Meat and Fish Preparation – Caribbean Style*, page 9.)
2. Remove the excess liquid.
3. With a sharp knife trim off any excess fat or sinew.
4. Season the oxtail pieces with the escallion, Scotch bonnet pepper, ginger, garlic, thyme, allspice, soy sauce, salt and pepper and leave to marinade in the refrigerator for at least 6 hours (or preferably overnight).
5. Remove the excess seasoning (from Step 4) prior to frying and set aside.
6. Add the oil to a Dutch Pot/frying pan and brown the oxtail pieces (without seasoning) for about 10 minutes.
7. Add the set aside seasoning, and stir in the water, onion and carrot, turn down the heat and cover the pot.
8. Simmer the oxtail for about 2–3 hours until it is tender (just falling off the bone) and the fat on the outside of the meat has been rendered down, stirring occasionally.
9. Remove the salted water/brine from the tinned/canned beans and add the beans to the pot.
10. Stir and simmer for a further 30 minutes.
11. Skim off excess liquid fat from the top of the dish and serve with rice and peas.

No. 11 STEW PEAS

(Non-Vegetarian)

Most likely to be found in: Jamaica.
Alternative Name: Stew Beef.

THE SECRET: This dish is usually ruined because it is too salty. Pickled pig tails are very salty, so you do not need to add salt to this dish. The more salt you can remove from the pickled pig's tails (or salt beef) prior to cooking, the better. *Remember* that you can always add more salt if necessary, but it is difficult to remove it if the pickled pig's tails (or salt beef) are too salty.

OTHER BACKGROUND INFORMATION: This dish has a very deceptive name as it is not a vegetarian dish, but rather a stew made from pickled and stewed meats. However, there is a vegetarian version of this dish called 'Stew Pigeon Peas'.

INGREDIENTS (SERVES 6):
450 g/1 lb pickled pig's tails, salt beef or ham hock*, diced
1 clove of garlic, crushed
2 cups red peas** (brown pigeon peas or kidney beans)
2 pints/1.1 litres approx. water (enough to cover meat)
225 g/½ lb stewing beef
1 x 400 ml tin/can coconut milk
1 tbsp Worcestershire sauce
2 escallion/green onion stalks
1 sprig of thyme
1 Scotch bonnet/hot pepper, chopped
1 small carrot, diced
15–20 boiled dumplings/spinners (see: Recipe No. 30)

METHOD:

*NB1: If pig's tails/beef have been preserved in salt water you need to soak them in fresh water for at least 6–8 hours (changing water regularly) to remove excess salt.

**NB2: Use tinned red peas to save time. Otherwise you will need to pre-soak and pre-cook dried peas prior to making this dish.

1. Bring to the boil the pig's tails, garlic and red peas in the water in a Dutch Pot/stock pot.
2. Reduce the heat and simmer until the meat is tender (1–1½ hours).
3. Prepare the stewing beef by trimming off any excess fat or sinew with a sharp knife.
4. Add the stewing beef to the pot.
5. Add the coconut milk, Worcestershire sauce, escallion, thyme, hot pepper, carrot and cook until the stewing beef is tender.
6. Make the dough for the dumplings/spinners and set aside (see: Recipe No. 30).
7. When the stewing beef is tender, make the dumplings/spinners and add to the pot.
8. Cook for a further 15 minutes and then remove from the heat.
9. Serve with boiled (plain) rice, and/or Ground Provisions.

No. 12 FRIED BAKE 'N' FISH

Most likely to be found: All over the eastern Caribbean.
Alternative Name: Shark n Bake.

THE SECRET: A light dough is achieved by using a quality instant yeast and allowing the dough to rest prior to frying. Do not allow salt to kill the yeast as your dough will not rise.

OTHER BACKGROUND INFORMATION: A very popular snack food, which can be served for breakfast or lunch by itself or with soup. In Trinidad & Tobago the preferred fish for this dish is shark. There was a time when the meat of the spiny dogfish shark (rock salmon) was widely available. However, this shark and eight other species have now been classified as endangered species.

INGREDIENTS (SERVES 6–8):
Bakes/Floats:
4 cups/600 g/20 oz flour
1½ tsp salt
4 tsp baking powder
2½ cups/600 ml/1 pint water
oil (for deep frying)

Fried Fish:
2 tbsp minced chive and thyme
1 tsp minced garlic
1 tsp salt
½ tsp pepper sauce
450 g/1 lb fish fillets (catfish, tilapia or shark)
2 limes, squeezed
2 tbsp flour
1–2 beaten eggs
breadcrumbs
oil (for frying)

METHOD:

Fried Bake:

1. Sift the flour, salt and baking powder into a bowl.
2. Add enough water to make a soft dough.
3. Knead for about 10 minutes.
4. Leave to rest for at least 30 minutes.
5. Divide the dough into 6–8 equal portions.
6. Flatten each portion to a diameter of 12.5–15 cm/5–6 inches and 0.5 cm/¼ inch thick.
7. If necessary, add flour or oil to your hands to prevent the dough from sticking.
8. Fry in hot oil until golden brown, turning once.
9. Remove the fried bake from the oil and place on kitchen towel to remove excess oil.

Fried Fish:

1. Make the seasoning: mix together the chive, thyme, garlic, salt, and pepper sauce.
2. Marinate the fish in the lime juice and seasoning for about 15–20 minutes.
3. Remove the excess seasoning/liquid.
4. Firstly dip the fish fillets in some flour, then the egg and finally in the breadcrumbs.
5. Shallow or deep fry the fillets on both sides until golden brown.
6. Remove the fillets from the frying pan and place on kitchen paper to remove excess oil.

To Assemble:

1. Slice the bake across the middle, but not the whole of the way through.
2. Insert a fillet and top with condiments and/or coleslaw.

No. 13 PIGEON PEAS & RICE

(NATIONAL DISH: ANGUILLA)

Most likely to be found: All over the Caribbean.
Alternative Names: Rice & Peas, Peas & Rice

THE SECRET: Fresh (green or brown) pigeon peas (as opposed to the canned or dried variety) make the most flavoursome dish. In Anguilla, this dish tastes best when you serve it immediately, garnished with sprigs of oregano.

OTHER BACKGROUND INFORMATION: Brown pigeon peas are also known as gungo peas and the green variety are known as 'Tropical Green Peas'. If you are unable to find fresh pigeon/gungo peas, why don't you try and grow your own as seeds are widely available? If buying the tinned/can variety online, search for 'Green Pigeon Peas' or 'Gungo Peas' (for the brown variety).

INGREDIENTS (SERVES 4):
1 x 400 g tin/can pigeon peas (or 100 g/4 oz dried
   or 250 g/9 oz fresh)
100 g/¼ lb salt beef (optional), chopped into small pieces
1½ cups/360 ml/12 fl oz water
2 cups/400 g/14 oz long grain rice
1 sprig of fresh thyme or 1 tsp dried thyme
1 tbsp butter
1 tsp hot pepper sauce
black pepper (to taste)
salt (to taste, only if you are not using salt beef!)

METHOD:

1. If using dried peas soak them overnight in a bowl of water.
2. If using fresh peas go to Step 4.
3. If using tinned peas go to Step 6.
4. Add fresh/rehydrated brown peas to a Dutch Pot/heavy-bottomed pan, and cover with water.
5. Bring the peas to the boil, reduce the heat and simmer until cooked.
6. Prepare the meat by removing any excess fat or sinew. Add the tinned peas to the pot/pan.
7. Brown the meat in a frying pan and then add to the cooked/tin peas in the pot/pan.
8. Add the water and bring to the boil.
9. Add the rice and seasonings, stir and bring back to the boil.
10. Reduce the heat and cover the pot/pan.
11. Simmer for about 20–30 minutes until all the liquid has been absorbed.
12. Taste and correct seasoning, and then serve.

No. 14 MACARONI PIE

Most likely to be found: All over the Caribbean.
Alternative Name: Mac 'n' Cheese.

THE SECRET: Do not over boil the macaroni. Use 100 per cent durum wheat macaroni as this will not be gummy when boiled. When cooked macaroni pie should be a solid mass, which can be cut into slices/cubes.

OTHER BACKGROUND INFORMATION: You can replace some of the milk with a chicken stock for extra flavour.

INGREDIENTS (SERVES 6):
1 packet of dried macaroni (500 g/20 oz approx)
2 tbsp butter
2 eggs
3 tsp tomato paste
¾ cup/180 ml/6 fl oz full fat milk
450 g/1 lb cheese (grated)
1 tsp parsley, chopped
1 sprig of chive, finely chopped
½ tsp paprika
1 tsp Angostura bitters
pepper sauce (to taste)
salt (to taste)

METHOD:

1. Boil the macaroni in water for about 10 minutes and then drain.
2. Add the butter into the hot macaroni and mix until melted.
3. Add the eggs, tomato paste, milk and most of the cheese, leaving some for sprinkling over in Step 5. Mix well.
4. Then add the herbs, paprika, bitters and pepper sauce and salt to taste, and mix well.
5. In a greased baking dish pour the mixture and sprinkle the remaining cheese over the top.
6. Sprinkle a small amount of paprika over the top of the pie.
7. Bake at 350°F/180°C/Gas Mark 4 for 30 minutes until firm and the top of the macaroni pie is golden brown.
8. Leave to cool for about 20 minutes, and then cut into cubes with a knife.
9. Serve with *Cucumber Chutney* (Recipe No. 70) and other Caribbean meat or fish dishes.

No. 15 ACKEE & SALT FISH
(NATIONAL DISH: JAMAICA)

Most likely to be found in: Jamaica.

THE SECRET: This dish is often ruined because either not enough salt has been removed from the salt fish prior to cooking or the salt fish is overcooked and becomes mushy. For best results soak the salted fish overnight, changing the water at least 3 or 4 times. Remember, you can always add more salt to taste, but you cannot correct an overly salted dish once it is cooked.

OTHER BACKGROUND INFORMATION: Salt fish (salted cod) is widely available in packaged and unpackaged forms in ethnic food stalls and markets, and also online. For more information see: *Salted Fish* in *Essential Caribbean Cooking Ingredients*, page 16.

INGREDIENTS (SERVES 4–6):
300 g/¾ lb dried salt fish (salted codfish)
2 tbsp oil
1 medium onion or 4 escallions, sliced
2 cloves of garlic, chopped
½ Scotch bonnet pepper, chopped or 2 tsp hot pepper sauce
3 slices of streaky bacon, chopped (optional)
3–4 medium sized tomatoes, chopped
1 x 400 g tin/can ackee (drained)
black pepper
2 sprigs of fresh thyme, chopped or 1 tsp dried thyme

METHOD:
Prepare Salt Fish:
1. If using dried salt fish: Soak the salt fish overnight in water or for at least 6–8 hours (changing the water at least 3–4 times) to remove excess salt.
2. If using tinned salt fish, go to Step 4.
3. Taste a small piece of the salt fish prior to use to check that it is not too salty. Change the water and soak for a further 2 hours, if necessary.
4. Drain the cod and cut or flake into small pieces using a fork.
5. Remove the bones and skin (if necessary) and then flake with a fork.

Cook Ackee & Salt Fish:
1. Heat the oil in a frying pan.
2. Sauté the onion/escallions until soft and light brown.
3. Add the garlic and Scotch bonnet pepper (or pepper sauce).
4. Add the bacon (optional) and stir.
5. Add the tomatoes, and cook for around 5 minutes, stirring occasionally.
6. Add the cod. Stir. Simmer for 5 minutes.
7. Add the can of drained ackee. Do not stir because this will cause the ackee to break up.
8. Cook for a few more minutes then sprinkle with black pepper and the thyme.

Serving:
Best served with a combination of Roasted Breadfruit, Johnny Cakes (Fried Dumplings – See: Recipe No. 16), Bammy, and/or fried or cooked plantains, cooked yams and/or sweet potatoes.

No. 16 FRIED DUMPLINGS (AND FESTIVALS)

Most likely to be found in: Jamaica.
Alternative Names: Floats, Johnny Cakes, Festivals (see: Other Background Information below), Cartwheels.

THE SECRET: Do not over fry or allow to dry out so that fried dumplings/bakes become as hard as cricket balls. Wrap in greaseproof paper to retain moisture.

OTHER BACKGROUND INFORMATION: Fried dumplings/ bakes vary widely from Caribbean island to island. From personal experience, we prefer them to be light and fluffy in the middle, which means more baking powder and less kneading.

Method 1 of this recipe can be adapted to create *'Festivals'* by (a) replacing the 2 cups of flour with ½ cup of cornmeal and 1½ cups of flour; (b) adding 3 tablespoons of sugar; (c) adding 1 teaspoon of vanilla essence; and then (d) rolling the dough into 2.5 cm/1 inch thick sausage shapes of 10–12.5 cm/4–5 inches in length before frying.

INGREDIENTS (SERVES 4–6):
2 cups/300 g/10 oz flour
2 tsp baking power
1 tbsp vegetable oil
½ cup/120 ml/4 fl oz cold water

METHOD:

1. Sieve the flour and baking power in a bowl.
2. Add enough water to the dry ingredients to make soft dough.
3. Knead the dough for about 10 minutes until it is a tight mass, and leave to rest for at least 30 minutes.
4. Divide the dough into 12 roughly equal pieces, and roll into balls.
5. Method 1: Flatten the dough balls until 0.5 cm/¼ inch thick and fry in hot oil that is at least half the height of the flattened dough balls, until golden brown, turning occasionally. Or:
6. Method 2: Fry the dough balls in hot oil that is at least half the height of the dough balls, until golden brown, turning occasionally.
7. Drain off excess oil using kitchen paper.
8. Serve with traditional Caribbean breakfast or other dishes.

No. 17 BREADFRUIT OIL DOWN

Most likely to be found: All over the Caribbean.
Alternative Names: Oil Down (Grenada and Trinidad & Tobago),
Run Down (Jamaica), Maetem Ghee (Guyana).

THE SECRET: The phrase 'oil down' refers to a dish being cooked in coconut milk until all of the milk has been absorbed, leaving a bit of coconut oil in the bottom of the pot. If you have cooked this dish correctly you will find your 'oil down' at the bottom of the pot.

OTHER BACKGROUND INFORMATION: Smoked ham, salt fish (cod) can be used as a substitute for salt beef or salted pig tails. The Trinidadian version uses a few different ingredients, such as Green Seasoning, which are not found in the Grenadian version, and does not contain callaloo leaves or saffron.

INGREDIENTS (SERVES 6):
1 large full breadfruit
225 g/8 oz pickled/salted meats (salted pig tails or salt beef)
2 tsp oil (for browning meat)
1 medium onion, sliced
1 stick of celery, sliced
2 sprigs of thyme
1 whole hot green pepper
2 blades of chive, chopped
1 sprig of parsley
5 cups/1.2 litres/2 pints coconut milk
8–10 callaloo leaves (optional – you can also use spinach if you
    cannot find callaloo)
2 tsp turmeric or 15 g/½ oz saffron or 2 tsp curry powder
½ tsp salt (to taste)
15–20 boiled dumplings/spinners (see: Recipe No. 30)

METHOD:

Roast Breadfruit:

1. **Warning:** Pierce the breadfruit with a fork or skewer, before placing it in the oven for roasting. Failure to do this could result in an explosion of the breadfruit causing possible damage to the oven and/or personal injury from the fruit's internal pressure.
2. Remove the stalk from the breadfruit and then roast/bake in a moderate oven at 350°F/180°C/Gas Mark 4 for about 1½–2 hours or until soft.

Prepare Oil Down:

1. Soak the salt meat for at least 24 hours, or overnight, to remove most of the salt, changing the water at least 3–4 times.
2. Heat the oil in a Dutch Pot or heavy-bottomed pan. Add the meat to the pot/pan.
3. Add the sliced onion, celery, thyme, pepper, chive and parsley and mix with the meat.
4. Slice the breadfruit in half, and then divide each half into two or three pieces to produce 1 cm/½ inch slices, peeling away the skin and core.
5. Place the breadfruit slices on top of the meat, making sure that they are not on top of each other.
6. Pour the coconut milk into the pot.
7. Wash the callaloo leaves, peel the stems and break the stems into pieces, and add to the pot (optional).
8. Spread the leaves open on the top of breadfruit, putting the smaller leaves between the larger ones.
9. Bring to the boil and then simmer.
10. Add the turmeric or saffron or curry powder and cook on medium heat for 50–60 minutes or until (a) the meat and breadfruit are tender, (b) the liquid is absorbed, and (c) the oil is visible around the sides of the breadfruit. Add salt to taste.
11. Make the dough for dumplings/spinners (see: Recipe No. 30) and add to the pot 10 minutes prior to the end of the cooking process.
12. Remove the excess oil and then serve.
13. Serve with avocado slices and a fresh fruit or milk drink.

No. 18 FILLED CHEESE SHELL

(National Dish: Aruba and Curaçao)

Most likely to be found in: Aruba and Curaçao.
Alternative Name: Keshi Yena (kay-shee-yay-na).

THE SECRET: Taking care not to pierce the shell when scooping out the middle of the cheese. **Curaçao Version**: There are *no eggs* in the Curaçao version and the dish is served cold.

OTHER BACKGROUND INFORMATION: Keshi Yena, literally translates to mean 'Stuffed Cheese'. An easier way of preparing this dish is to use cheese slices rather than scooping out a whole Edam/Gouda cheese. Then line the bottom and sides of an ovenproof dish with the slices, and fill the cheese with the meat mixture and cover with more cheese. Cooked shredded chicken can be used as a substitute for ground beef.

INGREDIENTS (SERVES 8–10):
1 whole Edam cheese (medium sized)

Filling Mixture:
2 tsp oil (for frying)
2 medium onions, diced
1 stick of celery with leaves, diced
3 tomatoes, peeled and chopped
1 large green pepper, chopped
900 g/2 lb ground beef or diced chicken breasts
2 tsp all-purpose Caribbean seasoning (or 1 stock cube)
1 cup/240 ml/8 fl oz water
1 tsp of ground white or black pepper
1 tbsp parsley, minced
1 bay leaf
Tabasco sauce – a few drops (optional)
¼ cup pimento olives, sliced
1 tbsp capers
¼ cup raisins
2 tbsp piccalilli
½ tsp tomato purée

2 tbsp tomato ketchup
½ tsp mustard (optional)
2 eggs, hard boiled, diced (optional – Curaçao version only)
2 eggs, beaten (optional – Curaçao version only)

METHOD:

(**NB:** The method below describes the Aruba version of this dish. Differences between this and the Curaçao version can be found in the *Other Background Information* section opposite.)

1. Remove the outer wax layer from the cheese.
2. Slice the top off the Edam cheese ball. Set lid aside for later.
3. With great care, hollow/scoop out the middle of the cheese, by using a small spoon. Ensure that the inside walls of the cheese are left intact with a 0.5–1 cm/¼–½ inch shell.
4. Add the oil to a large frying pan.
5. Sauté the onions, celery, tomatoes and green pepper.
6. Add the mince (or diced chicken) and stir into the other ingredients, until browned.
7. Add the seasoning (or stock cube), water, pepper, parsley, bay leaf, Tabasco sauce, pimento olives, capers, raisins and piccalilli.
8. Stir. Reduce heat, and then add the tomato purée, ketchup and mustard (optional). Stir again and cook for about 15–20 minutes. Take off the heat and leave to cool.
9. Preheat the oven to a medium heat (350°F/180°C/Gas Mark 4).
10. **Optional Step 1:** Stir the diced hard boiled eggs into the filling.
11. **Optional Step 2:** Stir half of the beaten eggs into the filling. Use the rest of the beaten egg to brush around the top of the cheese shell.
12. Add the cooled filling to the inside of the cheese shell.
13. Secure with the 'lid' that was removed earlier, brush with egg.
14. Grease a baking dish and fill it with about 3 cm/1 inch of water. Set the cheese in the dish and put in the oven for 1–1½ hours. The cheese will expand and flatten slightly but will keep its basic shape.
15. Serve piping hot, cut into wedges.

No. 19 SANCOCHO

(NATIONAL DISH: THE DOMINICAN REPUBLIC)

Most likely to be found in: The Dominican Republic,
Puerto Rico and many countries in Latin America.
Alternative Names: Latin Root Vegetable Stew,
Sancocho de Siete Carnes.

THE SECRET: 'Naranja Agria' is a sour orange widely used in
Dominican Republic cooking. This can be substituted by lemons.

OTHER BACKGROUND INFORMATION: It is almost impossible
to find a Sancocho recipe which everyone will agree upon, because
there are so many variations even within the regions of the Dominican
Republic. Sancocho is special occasion food, and families usually make
large batches. Simmered slowly, the vegetables break down somewhat to
thicken the stew.

In the Dominican Republic there is a variant of this dish called
Sancocho cruzado or *Sancocho de siete carnes* which includes chicken, beef,
pork, Longanizia (a type of pork sausage) and other meats. This dish
called *Sancocho de siete carnes* means *'Seven meat Sancocho'* and is
considered the ultimate sancocho dish.

INGREDIENTS (SERVES 6–8):
3 tbsp vegetable oil
3 large onions, diced
4 cloves of garlic, crushed
6 medium size tomatoes, chopped (or 1 x 400 g tin of
    chopped tomatoes)
1 litre/2 pints beef or chicken stock or water
450 g/1 lb beef, preferably with bones, diced
450 g/1 lb chicken, chopped
450 g/1 lb pork (or beef), diced
450 g/1 lb cassava, large dice
450 g/1 lb white yam, large dice
450 g/1 lb eddoes or yautia, large dice
225 g/½ lb potatoes, large dice
900 g/2 lb pumpkin, large dice
2 green bananas (figs), sliced

2 corn on the cob, sliced
1 sprig oregano or ½ tsp
salt and pepper (to taste)
2 x (Naranja Agria) sour oranges (or 2 large lemons), juiced
small bunch of coriander (cilantro)

METHOD:

1. Heat the oil in a Dutch Pot over medium heat.
2. Add the onions and sauté until translucent.
3. Add the garlic and stir.
4. Continue to stir and then add tomatoes.
5. Simmer the ingredients on medium heat until they are broken down.
6. Add the stock or water and meat and bring to the boil.
7. Reduce the heat to low and simmer for 30 minutes.
8. Add the root vegetables and simmer for another 30 minutes.
9. Add more stock or water if necessary.
10. Finally add the pumpkin, green bananas (figs), corn (cobs), oregano, salt and pepper and simmer until the meat is tender and the vegetables have begun to break down a bit (approximately 30–45 minutes.
11. Adjust the seasoning to taste and stir in the sour orange (lemon) juice and coriander (cilantro).
12. Serve hot with rice.

No. 20 DHAL PURI ROTI SKIN

Most likely to be found in: Trinidad & Tobago.
Alternative Name: Ground Split Peas Roti.

THE SECRET: The best dhal puri rotis are very light, soft and moist despite having a ground split pea filling. This is achieved by having a very fine dhal puri filling mix and not overworking the dough. Roti making is an art which takes many years of practice.

OTHER BACKGROUND INFORMATION: Before you try this recipe we suggest that you go onto YouTube and watch a few videos of authentic Trinidadian Dhal Puri Rotis being made.

INGREDIENTS (SERVES 8–10):
For Dough:
5 cups/750 g/25 oz plain flour
1 tbsp baking powder
½ tsp salt
525 ml/18.5 fl oz (approx) water, for kneading
60 ml/2 fl oz/¼ cup oil

For Filling:
1 cup yellow split peas
½ tsp saffron powder
½ tsp salt
3 cloves of garlic
1 small hot pepper
½ tsp ground cumin (geera)

For Cooking:
1 tbsp ghee or melted butter
120 ml/4 fl oz/½ cup oil

METHOD
Prepare Dough:
1. Sift the flour with the baking powder and salt.
2. Mix in enough water and knead the mixture to make a soft, stretchy dough.
3. Rub the oil over the dough.
4. Make a cut from the centre out to the edge and roll up the dough into a cone.
5. Press the peak and flatten the centre of the dough cone.
6. Leave to 'rest' for a further 20–30 minutes.
7. Once rested, roll out the dough (roti skin) again on a floured surface into thin circles of approximately 22.5 cm/9 inches in diameter (according to the size of your tawa).
8. Shape the dough into 8 or 10 even sized balls (loyahs).
9. Leave the dough balls (loyahs) to rest and prepare the filling.

Prepare Filling:
1. Boil the split peas until tender with the saffron, salt and *one* clove of garlic, and drain.
2. Grind the split peas (in electric blender or grinder) with a small hot pepper and the remaining 2 cloves of garlic.
3. **Tip 1:** If split peas are too moist to grind, remove excess water by drying out in the oven for 10 minutes.
4. Add the cumin and a little salt to taste. Mix and set aside. **Tip 2:** Completed Dhal Puri filling should have a fine texture, which will make it easier to fill the dough.

Fill Rotis:
1. Open up each ball of dough and place in the centre, 2–3 teaspoons of split peas as the filling.
2. Pull the sides of the dough over the split pea filling and close up the dough ball again. Turn over and leave to rest.
3. Roll out the dough ball with a rolling pin as thinly as possible, ensuring that none of the split pea filling falls out.

Cooking Rotis:
1. Heat the tawa on a medium heat.
2. Grease the tawa and place the rolled out roti on it.
3. Add the ghee (or butter) and oil to a bowl and use a wooden spoon to mix a smooth oily liquid.
4. Brush the top of the roti skin with the ghee or melted butter, cook for 1 minute on one side, turn over, and cook on the other side.
5. Be sure to press down the edges and any air pockets that may arise in the roti skin while cooking.
6. When the dhal puri roti is cooked and swells, remove from the tawa, fold and place on a tray, cover with greaseproof paper and allow to cool.
7. Serve with curried meat and/or vegetables.

No. 21 ANNA MARIA SALAD

(JAMAICAN STYLE)

Most likely to be found: All over the Caribbean.

THE SECRET: Fresh fruit and vegetables are the secret to this wonderfully simple salad that will have your guests coming back for more.

OTHER BACKGROUND INFORMATION: Can be served as part of lunch, dinner or as a snack. It's lovely with meat or fish.

INGREDIENTS (SERVES 12):
450 g/1 lb salad tomatoes
1 large cucumber
3 sweet, medium peppers (yellow, green and red)
1 whole pineapple
1 or 2 mangoes
2 x 198 g tins sweetcorn, drained (or 400 g frozen sweetcorn kernels, boiled and drained)
1 tsp brown sugar
½ tsp black pepper (ground)
4 tbsp tropical fruit juice

METHOD:
1. Wash the tomatoes, cucumber and peppers before using.
2. Peel and dice the pineapple.
3. Peel and dice the mangoes
4. Cut the tomatoes into small pieces
5. Prepare the sweetcorn.
6. Cut the cucumber into small pieces.
7. Deseed the peppers and chop into small pieces.
8. Put all the fruit and vegetables into a large bowl.
9. Add the sugar and black pepper to the fruit juice.
10. Mix everything and cover the bowl, then put in the fridge to chill for at least 1 hour.
11. Serve immediately.

No. 22 DOUBLES

Most likely to be found in: Trinidad & Tobago.
Alternative Names: Bara and Curried Channa,
Fried Flat Bread and Curried Chickpeas.

THE SECRET: Prior to cooking, the round Bara dough must be very thin, flat, oily and sticky to touch. If it is too heavy, dry or thick, the final Baras will have the wrong texture.

OTHER BACKGROUND INFORMATION: In Trinidad & Tobago Doubles are one of the most popular street foods, along with filled rotis. Bara (fried flat bread), like rotis and phulorie, originated in India. It takes two Baras to make up each Double and this is the reason for the name of this dish. As with Dhal Puri Roti Skin, it is probably worth going onto YouTube to watch a few videos of Trinidadian Doubles being made prior to trying this yourself.

INGREDIENTS (SERVES 6):
Bara (Fried Flat Bread):
2 cups/300 g/10 oz flour
½ tsp salt
¼ tsp sugar
1 tsp Trinidadian curry powder
1 tsp ground cumin (geera)
1 tsp saffron powder
½ tsp ground pepper
1 packet (7 g) of fast action dried yeast
5 fl oz/200 ml warm water (approx.)

Filling (Curried Channa – Chickpeas):
1 tbsp vegetable oil
1 medium onion, diced
3 cloves of garlic, minced
1 tbsp Trinidadian curry powder
1 x 400 g tin/can chickpeas
1 cup/240 ml/8 fl oz water
1 tsp ground cumin (geera)
1 tsp salt (to taste)

1 tsp black pepper (to taste)
1 tsp hot pepper sauce (to taste)

Cooking:
3 cups oil (for frying)

METHOD:
Make Bara Dough:
1. In a large bowl sieve the flour, salt, sugar, curry powder and ground cumin, saffron powder and ground pepper.
2. Add the dried yeast.
3. Add enough warm water to the flour mixture to make a slightly firm dough.
4. Mix well, but try to handle the dough as little as possible.
5. Cover the dough with a damp cloth and allow to rise until it doubles in size (approximately 1–1½ hours).
6. Prepare the filling while waiting for the dough to rise.

Make Channa Filling:
1. Heat the oil in a heavy frying pan.
2. Add the diced onion, minced garlic and 1 tablespoon of Trinidadian curry powder pre-mixed with ¼ cup of water.
3. Sauté the onion for a few minutes, and then add the chickpeas to the pan.
4. Stir the ingredients ensuring that the chickpeas are well coated in the curry sauce and then cook for a further 5 minutes.
5. Add 1 cup water, 1 teaspoon of cumin, and salt and pepper (to taste) to the pan.
6. Reduce to medium heat, cover the pan and allow the ingredients to simmer for 20–35 minutes until the chickpeas are soft. (Taste a single chickpea at 5 minute intervals after 20 minutes to see whether they are cooked.)
7. The cooked chickpea filling should be soft and moist, so add more water to the curry sauce if necessary.
8. Add hot pepper sauce to taste if required prior to serving.

Frying Bara:
1. With a knife cut the dough into a number of even pieces (8, 10 or 12 pieces) and then roll into an even number of dough balls.
2. Before handling the dough balls any further use oil to moisten the palms of your hands to prevent sticking.
3. Pat the dough balls into individual 10–12.5 cm/ 4–5 inch flat circles using both hands.
5. Allow the flattened dough circles to rest for around 10–15 minutes prior to cooking.
5. Heat the oil in a Dutch Pot/heavy-bottomed pan (or fryer) – to around 170°C.
6. Deep fry the Baras in hot oil until puffy (about 15–20 seconds per side), turn once and then place on kitchen paper to remove excess oil.

Serving:
1. Serve when all the Baras are cooked.
2. Add 1 tablespoon of curried chickpeas to the base of one Bara, top with 1 teaspoon of your favourite chutney or sauce (Cucumber Chutney (Recipe No. 70) hot pepper sauce or mango chutney) and then cover another Bara on top for a sandwich.

No. 23 FRIED PLANTAIN

Most likely to be found: All over the Caribbean.
Alternative Name: Plantain Banana.

THE SECRET: ★When you buy your plantains, make sure the plantains are yellow ripe with dark spots. The more yellow the plantains are, the better they are for frying. Do *not* buy plantain with completely black skin as they are over ripe and may make you ill if fried.

OTHER BACKGROUND INFORMATION: Plantain is a green to yellow boat shaped fruit (shade of colour depends on the stage of ripening) and is a close relative of the banana. It looks like a banana, but is bigger, longer and has a thicker skin. Unlike bananas, plantain needs to be cooked before eaten.

INGREDIENTS (SERVES 6):
3 plantains (ripe★)
3 tbsp vegetable oil

METHOD:
1. Wash the skins of the plantains in cold water to remove dirt.
2. Using a sharp knife, make an incision along the entire length of each plantain.
3. Slide your first finger along the incision and remove the skin.
4. Place the peeled plantain on a cutting board and cut it into 0.5 cm/¼ inch pieces at a 45 degree angle.
5. Heat 1 tbsp of the oil in a frying pan, and then reduce the heat to medium.
6. Carefully place the pieces of one plantain into the warm oil.
7. Let the pieces fry until they turn light brown around the edges and then turn over to allow the other side to brown.
8. Fry the plantain pieces for approximately 1 minute more.
9. Remove them from the frying pan and place on paper towel to remove excess oil.
10. Repeat Steps 5–9 for the second and third plantain.
11. Serve as a snack or side dish for breakfast, lunch or dinner with most Caribbean dishes.

No. 24 ESCOVITCH FISH

Most likely to be found in: Jamaica.
Alternative Name: Fried Fish in Pickled Liquor/Sauce.

THE SECRET: The secret of a good Escovitch fish is to ensure that the fish is not over fried (otherwise it will be hard and chewy) and that the vinegar liquor is not too strong. If it is too strong it will overpower the natural flavours of the fish. (**Tip:** Try using a combination of white wine vinegar and lemon/lime juice for a more delicately flavoured liquor.)

OTHER BACKGROUND INFORMATION: *Escovitch* is a cooking process whereby fish is fried, and then covered with a pickled liquor made from vinegar, pimenta, onions, pepper, and carrots (optional).

Which Caribbean Fish? ★Hake, Red Snapper, King Fish, Red Mullet, Grey Mullet, Coley, Tilapia and Trevally are the most popular for Caribbean fish dishes.

INGREDIENTS (SERVES 6):
5 whole medium sized Caribbean fish★/10 Caribbean fish
     steaks★ (see: *Which Caribbean Fish?* above) cleaned, with the
     heads and tails left on
2 fresh limes, squeezed, or 2 tbsp lime juice (optional)
2 tsp Jamaican/Caribbean fish seasoning
3 cloves of garlic, crushed
1½ tsp black pepper
Oil, for shallow frying
2 onions
1 sweet red pepper
1 sweet green pepper
1 Scotch bonnet pepper or 2 tsp hot pepper sauce
1 carrot (optional)
5 pimenta berries (allspice) or 1 tsp ground pimenta
3 tbsp white vinegar or white wine vinegar

METHOD:
Prepare Fish:
1. Prepare the fish using the lime juice (optional). (See: *Meat and Fish Preparation – Caribbean Style*, page 9.)
2. Remove the excess liquid.
3. With a sharp knife cut small deep gashes on each side of the fish.
4. Rub the fish seasoning, crushed garlic and black pepper on the outside and in the cavities of the fish and then place in a bowl.
5. Place the bowl in the refrigerator and allow the fish to marinade there for at least 1 hour.
6. Place some oil in a Dutch Pot/fryer and heat up slowly to around 175°C.
7. Carefully place the fish portions into the Dutch Pot/fryer and shallow fry for 3–5 minutes each side until the skin is crisp and golden brown.
8. Cover the Dutch Pot/fryer with the lid to reduce frying smell.
9. Turn over the fish and fry the other side.
10. Remove the fish from the pot/fryer and place on kitchen towels to remove excess oil.

Prepare Vegetables and Escovitch Liquor/Sauce:
1. Slice the onions, sweet and hot peppers, and carrot.
2. Add 1 teaspoon of oil to a frying pan.
3. Add the onions and fry for 3 minutes.
4. Add the peppers and carrot to the onions and fry for a further 2 minutes.
5. Reduce the heat then add the ground pimenta and vinegar to the frying pan.
6. Cover the ingredients in the frying pan and allow to simmer (to reduce) for 4–6 minutes then remove from the heat.
7. Place the fried fish into a serving bowl/dish.
8. Pour the vegetables and the hot liquor over the top of the fried fish and allow to soak into fish.
9. Serve with fried dumplings, fried plantain and rice and peas.

No. 25 FRIED FISH

Most likely to be found: All over the Caribbean.

THE SECRET: The secret of good fried fish is ensuring that it is not fried for too long (otherwise it will be hard and chewy). If in doubt it is better to slightly under fry the fish and then place in the oven on medium heat for a few minutes afterwards to complete the cooking process.

OTHER BACKGROUND INFORMATION: Readymade Caribbean fish seasonings are now widely available in ethnic food stores or on the internet. However, they tend to contain too much salt (sodium chloride) so you may wish to make your own version by combining 1 teaspoon of the following ingredients in equal measure: pimenta seeds, fennel, garlic, black pepper, celery, cumin, ginger, coriander, sugar. Or 2 teaspoons of light soya sauce can be used as an alternative to salt.

INGREDIENTS (SERVES 4–6):
4–6 medium sized snapper fish
3–4 tbsp vinegar/lime juice (optional)
2 tsp Caribbean fish seasoning
3 tsp ground black pepper
3 cups oil (for deep frying fish)
2 tsp oil (for shallow frying vegetables)
1 small green sweet pepper, thinly sliced
1 small red sweet pepper, thinly sliced
1 small yellow sweet pepper, thinly sliced
1 medium onion, thinly sliced
1 carrot, thinly sliced (optional)
1 freshly squeezed lime (or 2 tsp lime juice) for vegetables

METHOD:

1. Prepare the fish using the vinegar/lime juice (optional). (See: *Meat and Fish Preparation – Caribbean Style*, page 9.)
2. Remove the excess liquid.
3. With a sharp knife cut small deep gashes on each side of the fish. Rub the fish seasoning and black pepper on the outside and in the cavities of the fish and then place in a bowl.
4. Place the bowl in the refrigerator and allow the fish to marinate there for at least 1 hour.
5. Place the oil in a Dutch Pot/frying pan and heat up slowly to around 175°C.
6. Fry the fish in the Dutch Pot/fryer for 4–7 minutes (depending on the size of the fish) until golden brown.
7. Cover the Dutch Pan/fryer with the lid to reduce frying smell.
8. Remove the fish from the oil and place on kitchen towel/paper to remove excess oil.
9. In a frying pan heat a little oil and add the peppers, onion and carrot (optional).
10. Sauté the vegetables in the pan and add lime juice when they are almost cooked.
11. Garnish the fish with the vegetables and serve.

No. 26 GRILLED FISH
WITH SAUCE AU CHIEN

(NATIONAL DISH: MARTINIQUE)

Most likely to be found in: Martinique
and other islands of the Caribbean.
Alternative Name: Grilled Snapper in Creole (Vinaigrette) Sauce.

THE SECRET: This is a very simple dish with no great secrets.
However with all fish dishes it is important not to under or overcook
the fish.

OTHER BACKGROUND INFORMATION: Martinique cooking is
very much influenced by French foods, blending African, Asian and
European influences into mouth watering French Creole creations.

INGREDIENTS (SERVES 4):
For Fish:
4 fresh snappers, cleaned and washed
2 tbsp vinegar (optional)
2 tsp lime juice (optional)
2 tsp Caribbean fish seasoning (optional)
2 tbsp flour (for seasoning)
2 tbsp oil

For Sauce:
1 medium onion, finely chopped
1 medium tomato, finely chopped
3 escallions, finely chopped
3 cloves of garlic, minced
1 Scotch bonnet pepper, deseeded and finely chopped or
    1–2 tsp hot pepper sauce (to taste)
3 sprigs fresh basil, finely chopped
3 sprigs fresh parsley, finely chopped
1 tsp black pepper
1 cup/240 ml/8 fl oz boiling water
¼ cup/60 ml/2 fl oz olive oil
¾ cup/180 ml/6 fl oz cider/wine vinegar
1 tbsp Dijon mustard

1 fresh lime or 2 tbsp lime juice
2 egg yolks, hard boiled and then mashed
½ tsp salt (to taste)

METHOD:
Prepare Snapper:
1. Prepare the fish using the vinegar/lime juice (optional). (See: *Meat and Fish Preparation – Caribbean Style*, page 9.)
2. Remove the excess liquid.
3. Season the fish with salt and pepper, or fish seasoning (optional).
4. Coat each fish lightly with flour, tapping off the excess.
5. Oil the rack and grill the fish over a moderately hot flame until cooked through, about 5 minutes per side.

Prepare Creole (Vinaigrette) Sauce:
1. Combine the chopped onion, tomato, escallion, garlic, Scotch bonnet pepper/pepper sauce, basil, parsley, and black pepper in a bowl.
2. Add enough boiling water to the bowl in order to cover the ingredients and then it let stand so that the flavours blend.
3. In a separate bowl, add the olive oil, vinegar, mustard, and lime juice and then whisk together to make the vinaigrette.
4. Add the chopped egg yolks to the vinaigrette, and then stir into the onion-pepper mixture and combine well.
5. Add salt to taste.
6. Let the sauce stand, uncovered, at room temperature for at least 1 hour before serving.

Serving:
1. Place the cooked fish on a plate/platter and then pour over 1–2 tablespoons of the sauce.
2. Serve with rice, vegetables or salad.

No. 27 FRIED BAKES (FLOAT) & SALT FISH

Most likely to be found: All over the eastern Caribbean.
Alternative Names: Hot Bakes and Salt Fish Buljol, Float and Salt Fish.

THE SECRET: The dough must not be overworked, and must be allowed to rest before frying. Fried Bakes should be soft, very light and not too greasy.

OTHER BACKGROUND INFORMATION: In many ways Fried Bakes are similar to Jamaican Fried Dumplings, but they tend to be lighter and softer. You need to soak the dried salt fish for several hours or overnight before preparing the rest of the dish. However, tinned salt fish (not as widely available) can be used straight from the can without pre-soaking. See page 16.

INGREDIENTS (SERVES 6):
Fried Bake:
450 g/1 lb plain/all-purpose flour
1 tbsp sugar
5 tsp baking powder
½ tsp salt
¼ cup/60 ml/2 fl oz milk
1 cup/240 ml/8 fl oz water
oil (for deep frying)

Salt Fish Filling:
1 packet (400 g) of dried, boneless salt fish (or 2 x 185 g
   boneless tinned salt fish)
1 tsp oil (for frying)
1 medium onion, finely diced
2 cloves of garlic, crushed, or 1 tsp garlic powder
1 tsp black pepper, grounded
1 sweet pepper, finely diced
1 medium tomato, finely diced with seeds removed

METHOD:
Fried Bakes:
1. Pour the flour into a large bowl add the sugar, baking powder and salt. Mix thoroughly and add the milk and water.
2. Knead the dough until it becomes soft and almost sticky to the touch. If it becomes too sticky, add a little flour and knead the dough until you can touch it.
3. When you have finished kneading the dough, cover it with a damp cloth/tea towel and allow it to rise for at least 30 minutes.
4. Heat a frying pan, and then pour oil into it.
5. Cut up the dough into small balls and flatten them so they are about 1 cm/½ inch thick.
6. Place them into your frying pan of hot oil on a medium heat until they have turned golden brown. Then turn them over to cook the other side.

Salt Fish (Buljol):
1. If using dried salt fish: Soak the salt fish overnight in water or for at least 6–8 hours (changing the water every 2 hours) to remove excess salt.
2. If used tinned salt fish: Go to Step 5.
3. Taste a small piece of the salt fish prior to use to check that it is not too salty. Change the water and soak for a further 2 hours, if necessary.
4. Strain off water from the salt fish and flake in a bowl, and then set aside.
5. Add the oil to a frying pan, then sauté the onion for 3-4 minutes.
6. Add the garlic, black pepper, diced sweet pepper and tomato to the pan.
7. Flake the salt fish with a fork or dice with a sharp knife.
8. Once the sweet pepper is cooked, add the salt fish and heat through for 3-4 minutes.
9. Remove from the heat and set aside.

Serving:
Cut a pocket on the side of the hot/fried bake and add the salt fish mixture, then serve.

No. 28 GREEN FIG & SALT FISH PIE

(NATIONAL DISH: ST LUCIA)

Most likely to be found: All over the Caribbean.
Alternative Name: Fig Vét é Lanmowi.

THE SECRET: Green Figs (unripe green bananas) are the key ingredients for this dish. They are now more widely available in ethnic food stores and markets. *Do not* confuse with plantain.

OTHER BACKGROUND INFORMATION: This dish is prepared for breakfast and can be served as a pie, or a non-pie form by missing out the 'Prepare Pie' steps. You need to soak the dried salt fish for several hours or overnight before preparing the rest of the dish. However, tinned salt fish (not as widely available) can be used straight from the can without pre-soaking. For more information see: *Salted Fish* in *Essential Caribbean Cooking Ingredients*, page 16.

INGREDIENTS (SERVES 6):
450 g/1 lb salt fish
900 g/2 lb green figs (green bananas)
1 tbsp lime juice or 1 fresh lime
2 sweet peppers, cut into thin strips
1 onion, thinly sliced
2 tomatoes, thinly sliced
225 g/½ lb cheese, grated
½ tsp black pepper
½ cup/120 ml/4 fl oz milk
1 tsp breadcrumbs

METHOD:
Prepare Salt Fish and Green Figs:
1. If using dried salt fish: Soak the salt fish overnight in water or for at least 6–8 hours (changing the water every 2 hours) to remove excess salt.
2. If using tinned salt fish: Go to Step 4.
3. Taste a small piece of the salt fish prior to use to check that it is not too salty. Change the water and soak for a further 2 hours, if necessary.
4. Cut the green figs in half, but do not remove the skin.
5. Place the green figs in a pan of boiling water and cook until tender (15–20 minutes).
6. Drain off the water, peel and crush the green figs with a fork while they are still hot.
7. Sprinkle the crushed green figs with the lime juice to prevent them going dark, and set aside.
8. Flake the salt fish with a fork (or dice with a sharp knife) and set aside.

Prepare Pie
1. Press half of the crushed figs in a greased baking pie dish.
2. Sprinkle half of the shredded fish on the figs.
3. Spread half of the sweet peppers, onion, tomatoes, cheese and black pepper on the figs.
4. Repeat the layer – beginning with green fig and ending with grated cheese and black pepper.
5. Top with the milk and sprinkle with the breadcrumbs.
6. Bake in an oven at 350°F/180°C/Gas Mark 4, for 30–40 minutes or until the cheese has melted and is golden brown.
7. Serve.

No. 29 STEWED SALT FISH WITH COCONUT DUMPLINGS, SPICY PLANTAINS & BREADFRUIT

(NATIONAL DISH: ST KITTS & NEVIS)

Most likely to be found in: St Kitts & Nevis.

THE SECRET: This is a relatively simple dish but with lots of elements, so it requires a bit of preplanning to get it right.

OTHER BACKGROUND INFORMATION: If you are roasting a whole breadfruit you should do this the day before as it takes time to cool down. For best results fry your breadfruit segments when they are cold. See page 16 for preparing the salt fish.

INGREDIENTS (SERVES 6):

1 large full breadfruit – enough when chopped into
    2.5 cm/1 inch pieces to fill 3 cups, see: Seasoned
    Breadfruit, opposite

Stewed Salt Fish:
450 g/1 lb salt fish (dried or tinned)
4 tbsp vegetable oil
1 green pepper, diced
6 escallions, finely chopped
1 small onion, chopped
5 cloves of garlic, chopped
450 g/1 lb tomatoes, chopped
2 tbsp margarine
salt and pepper (to taste)
2 tbsp parsley, chopped

Spicy Plantains:
3 medium sized plantains, peeled and chopped into 1 cm/½
    inch pieces
¼ tsp hot sauce or 1 Scotch bonnet pepper, chopped and
    deseeded
¼ tsp salt

2 tbsp fresh ginger, peeled and grated
1 small onion, grated
oil (for frying)

Coconut Dumplings:
1½ cups/225 g/7½ oz flour
½ cup grated coconut
¼ tsp salt
1 tbsp margarine
1 tbsp oil
½ cup/120 ml/4 fl oz water

Seasoned Breadfruit:
1 tbsp unsalted butter or margarine
2 tbsp oil
1 medium onion, chopped
4 cloves of garlic, crushed
1 tbsp chopped fresh thyme leaves
½ cup sweet red pepper, diced
2 tbsp fresh parsley, chopped
3 cups breadfruit chopped into 2.5 cm/1 inch pieces
1 cup/240 ml/8 fl oz chicken broth/stock
¼ tsp salt (to taste)
¼ tsp freshly ground black pepper (to taste)

METHOD:
Roast Breadfruit:
1. **Warning:** Pierce the breadfruit with a fork or skewer, before placing it in the oven for roasting. Failure to do this could result in an explosion of the breadfruit causing possible damage to the oven and/or personal injury from the fruit's internal pressure.
2. Remove the stalk from the breadfruit and then roast/bake in a moderate oven at 350°F/180°C/Gas Mark 4 for about 1½–2 hours or until soft. When cold, chop into 2.5 cm/1 inch pieces discarding skin and core.

Stewed Salt Fish
1. If using dried salt fish: Soak the salt fish overnight in water or for at least 6–8 hours (changing the water every 2 hours) to remove salt.
2. If using tinned salt fish: Go to Step 5.

3. Taste a small piece of the salt fish prior to use to check that it is not too salty. Change the water and soak for a further 2 hours, if necessary.
4. Flake the salt fish with a fork (or dice with a sharp knife) and set aside.
5. Heat the oil in a large heavy saucepan. Add the pepper, escallions, onion and garlic.
6. Cover and cook over low heat for 5 minutes, stirring occasionally.
7. Add the tomatoes and simmer over moderate heat until heated through for about 2–3 minutes.
8. Add the flaked/diced salt fish along with the margarine, salt and pepper. Cover the stew and simmer over low heat until heated through for about five minutes.
9. Arrange the salt fish on a plate. Sprinkle with the parsley and serve with dumplings, breadfruit and spicy plantains.

Spicy Plantain – Preparation:
1. Combine all the ingredients in a bowl. Toss until mixed.
2. Fry in batches in the oil until golden brown and cooked.
3. Remove and drain on paper towels.
4. Serve alongside the salt fish, dumplings and breadfruit.

Coconut Dumplings – Preparation:
1. Place the flour, coconut, salt, margarine and oil in a bowl.
2. Gradually stir in the water to make a stiff dough.
3. Turn onto a lightly floured board and knead for about 2 minutes.
4. Make the dumplings into the desired shape. Slide the dumplings into boiling salted water.
5. Cover and cook for about 10–15 minutes.

Fry Breadfruit – Preparation:
1. Melt the butter or margarine in a heavy saucepan over medium heat then add the oil.
2. Add the onion and cook until golden about 5–8 minutes, stirring often.
3. Add the garlic, thyme, red pepper and parsley and sauté for 30 seconds.
4. Remove from the heat and add the breadfruit with the chicken broth or other prepared liquid.
5. Toss gently to blend and heat through. Season to taste with salt and pepper. Serve with the dumplings, salt fish and spicy plantain.

No. 30 BOILED DUMPLINGS

(FOR SOUP AND STEWS)

Most likely to be found: All over the Caribbean.
Alternative Names: Spinners, Sinkers, Dumplings.

THE SECRET: For best results you must leave the dough to rest prior to adding to a dish, otherwise the cooked dumplings will be hard and difficult to chew.

OTHER BACKGROUND INFORMATION: Use cold meat or vegetable stock as a substitute for water to get extra flavour.

INGREDIENTS (FOR 15–20 SMALL DUMPLINGS):
225 g/8 oz plain/all-purpose flour
½ tsp salt (to taste)
1 cup/240 ml/8 fl oz water or milk

METHOD:
1. Sieve the four and salt into a mixing bowl.
2. Slowly add the water and knead into a stiff dough.
3. Cover and let rest for about 30 minutes.
4. Pinch a 15 g/½ oz piece of dough.
   Either:
   a) Roll each piece of dough into a long thin rope in the palm of your hands to make spinners; or
   b) Roll each piece of dough into a small ball and then flatten into 5 cm/2 inch discs to make round dumplings.
5. Drop the dough pieces into simmering soup or stew. Stir and cook 10–15 minutes before serving.

No. 31 COU-COU & FLYING FISH

(National Dish: Barbados)

Most likely to be found in: Barbados and Anguilla.

THE SECRET: Bajan seasoning and the herb marjoram are two ingredients used to make authentic Barbadian (Bajan) dishes.

OTHER BACKGROUND INFORMATION: Barbados is known throughout the Caribbean as the *land of the flying fish*.

Flying fish are a species of fish that, if necessary to avoid a predator, can make very powerful, self-propelled leaps out of water into air using their long, wing-like fins to enable them to glide for considerable distances above the water's surface. They tend to live in warm tropical oceans such as the Caribbean.

Flying fish have a very special place in Barbadian (Bajan) culture as they are depicted on everything from artwork, coins, to fountain sculptures and form part of the official Barbados Tourism Authority logo.

INGREDIENTS (SERVES 6):
For Cou-Cou:
2 cups cornmeal (polenta – fine or medium)
2 cups/480 ml/16 fl oz cold water (for soaking cornmeal)
7 (fingers) okras, finely sliced
1 tsp salt
1 medium onion, finely chopped
3 cloves of garlic, crushed/minced
2 sprigs of thyme, finely diced/minced
4 cups/960 ml/32 fl oz boiling water (for boiling okras)
1 tbsp butter/margarine
1 tbsp oil

For Flying Fish:
8 flying fish fillets
1 tbsp salt
3 limes, squeezed
3 tbsp Bajan seasoning
3 tbsp margarine
1 large onion, sliced

6 cloves of garlic, minced
1 large tomato, chopped
1 tsp parsley, chopped
15 g/½ oz fresh thyme
15 g/½ oz fresh marjoram
1 green pepper, cut in julienne strips
1 tsp lime juice
2 cups/480 ml/16 fl oz water
½ tsp hot pepper sauce
½ tsp curry powder
½ tsp salt (to taste)

METHOD:
For Cou-Cou:
1. Soak the cornmeal in cold water for 5 minutes.
2. Combine the okras, salt, onion, garlic and thyme in a saucepan.
3. Add the water to the pan, and bring to the boil.
4. Reduce the heat and let simmer for 10 minutes.
5. Remove the pan from the heat and strain off the water from the okras, setting aside the okra liquid and cooked okras.
6. In a thick-bottomed saucepan, over a low flame, put the soaked cornmeal and half of the okra liquid. Stir constantly with a whisk.
7. Add in stages the remaining okra liquid.
8. Continue to stir and allow to steam until the cornmeal is totally cooked.
9. Add the okra, butter/margarine and oil. Mix well and serve with the flying fish.

For Steamed Flying Fish:
1. Marinate the fish in salt and lime juice for 10 minutes.
2. Rinse the fish and pat dry with paper towels, and then rub in the Bajan seasoning and leave to marinate for 1 hour.
3. Roll each fish into a sausage shape, starting with the tail.
4. Heat the margarine in a saucepan and sauté the onion and garlic until the onion becomes transparent.
5. Add the tomato and parsley and continue to cook for 2 minutes.
6. Tie the thyme and marjoram together and add to the pan together with the remaining ingredients.
7. Place the rolled fish on the mixture in the pan, reduce the heat, cover and simmer for 10 minutes until the fish is cooked.

No. 32 STEWED PIGEON PEAS

Most likely to be found in: The eastern Caribbean.
Alternative Name: Stew Peas.

THE SECRET: This is a very simple dish but needs to be seasoned well to have a good flavour. Replace water with vegetable stock to improve flavour.

OTHER BACKGROUND INFORMATION: Stewed Pigeon Peas is served as part of Sunday dinner on many eastern Caribbean islands. The brown variety of pigeon peas are called 'gungo peas'.

INGREDIENTS (SERVES 6):
2 cups brown pigeon peas (fresh) or 2 x 400 g tins/cans
   brown pigeon peas
4 cups water
3 tbsp oil
2 tbsp brown sugar
1 onion, finely diced
3 escallions, finely diced
4 cloves of garlic, crushed/minced
3 sprigs of thyme, finely diced
2 tbsp Green Seasoning
½–1 tsp salt (to taste)
1 tsp hot pepper (to taste)

METHOD:

Note: If you are using fresh pigeon peas these need to be soaked overnight and then cooked for 1–1½ hours prior to starting this dish. (Do *not* throw away the dark water in which the peas have been boiled, as this will be added back into the dish later.) Taste the peas to check whether they are cooked.

1. Remove all water from the peas, and set the water to one side.
2. In a Dutch Pot/heavy-bottomed pan heat the oil and brown sugar over high heat until the sugar caramelizes by rising to the surface. (**NB:** Caramelized sugar should be dark brown, but not burnt.)
3. Add the diced onion, escallions and garlic to the caramelized sugar and stir quickly for 1 minute.
4. Add the peas, thyme and Green Seasoning and reduce the heat.
5. Add the pea water and cook on medium heat for 15 minutes, stirring occasionally.
6. Add the salt and hot pepper to taste.
7. Serve with white rice, Caribbean meat/fish dishes and salad.

No. 33 CRACK CONCH WITH PEAS & RICE

(National Dish: The Bahamas)

Most likely to be found in: The Bahamas.
Alternative Name: Fried Sea Snail with Rice and Peas.

THE SECRET: Fresh conch (pronounced 'konk') meat is secret to this dish. Prawns and/or crayfish can be used as a substitute if you are unable to find conch meat at your local fishmonger. Do not over fry as the conch flesh will become too chewy.

OTHER BACKGROUND INFORMATION: This dish is sometimes served with optional side dishes of potato salad, macaroni cheese (Bahamian style – so thick, you can cut it like cake, with a knife), coleslaw and fried plantains.

Conch is a medium to large sea snail that lives in a large shell in tropical waters. Removing the conch meat from its shell is a very specialist task, so you should ask your fishmonger to do this.

INGREDIENTS (SERVES 6):

For Rice and Peas
2 slices bacon/salt pork, diced
1 onion, diced
1 Scotch bonnet pepper, diced and seeds removed (or 1 tsp of hot pepper sauce)
12 ripe tomatoes, chopped
12 cups tomato paste
2 tsp chopped fresh thyme
1 x 400 g can/tin pigeon peas (brown or green varieties)
1½ cups/300 g/10½ oz long grain rice

For Tempura Batter
450 g/1 lb flour
1 egg (beaten)
1 tsp black pepper
1 tsp garlic powder
1 sprig of fresh thyme
2–4 cups/480–960 ml/16–32 fl oz water

For Conch/Crayfish:
450 g/1 lb conch (sea snail flesh, removed from its shell)
oil (for frying)

METHOD:
Prepare Rice and Peas:
1. Fry the bacon or salt pork in a large pan with a tight-fitting lid.
2. Add the onion, hot pepper, tomatoes, tomato paste and thyme, followed by the peas, salt and pepper to taste.
3. Add 3 cups of water to the mix and bring to a boil.
4. Add the rice and stir.
5. Cover and cook on medium heat for about 30 minutes or until the rice is tender and the water is absorbed.
6. Set aside and prepare the Crack Conch.

Prepare Tempura Batter:
1. Mix the flour, beaten egg, seasonings and water into a batter, making sure you add the water slowly since the batter should not be too watery but should be of a paste like consistency.

Prepare Crack Conch:
1. Clean the conch for cooking.
2. Bruise (pound) with a metal mallet until very tender.
3. Dip the conch in the batter and then deep fry or grill until golden brown.
4. Place the cooked conch on kitchen towel to remove excess oil.
5. Serve with the Rice and Peas.

No. 34 MOUNTAIN CHICKEN
(FROGS' LEGS)

(NATIONAL DISH: DOMINICA)

Most likely to be found in: Dominica, Trinidad & Tobago.
Alternative Names: Crapo, Crapaud.

THE SECRET: Do not over fry the frogs' legs as this will make them hard and rubbery.

OTHER BACKGROUND INFORMATION: Mountain chicken can be found also in Montserrat, and is more in abundance at certain times of year in Dominica than at other times.

INGREDIENTS (SERVES 6–8):
For Meat:
6–8 or 12–16 frogs' legs (crapaud)
2 tbsp vinegar (optional)
1 lime, squeezed (optional)
2 cloves of garlic
¼ tsp chopped thyme
¼ tsp hot pepper sauce
½ cup flour
½ cup oil (for frying)

For Gravy:
1 tbsp oil
1 tbsp butter
1 small onion, diced
2 tbsp flour
1 cup/240 ml/8 fl oz water

For Ground Provisions:
4 green bananas, peeled and sliced
2 dasheen, peeled and cut into equal size pieces
2 medium sized yams, peeled and cut into equal size pieces
½ tsp salt
1 green pepper, sliced

METHOD:

1. Prepare the frogs' legs using the vinegar/lime juice (optional). (See: *Meat and Fish Preparation – Caribbean Style*, page 9.).
2. Remove the excess liquid.
3. With a sharp knife trim off any excess fat, skin or sinew.
4. Place the frogs' legs in a bowl and add the garlic, thyme and hot pepper sauce.
5. Marinate the frogs' legs in the refrigerator for at least 2–3 hours, to allow the seasoning to be absorbed.
6. Pat the legs dry with kitchen towel, then roll in the flour and prepare to fry.
7. Heat the oil slowly to around 175°C.
8. Place the legs in the hot oil and fry until golden brown.
9. Place on kitchen towel/paper to remove excess oil.

Gravy Preparation:

1. Heat the oil and butter in a large saucepan.
2. Add the onion and sauté for 3–4 minutes.
3. Add the flour and stir to create a smooth paste (roux).
4. Slowly stir in the water, and then bring the gravy to the boil.
5. Reduce the heat and simmer for approximately 5 minutes.
6. Add the legs to the pot of gravy. Stir and simmer for a further 5 minutes.
7. Remove the pot from the heat and allow to stand.

Ground Provisions Preparation:

1. Peel and clean the provisions (green bananas, dasheen and yams), and boil in salt water.
2. Add the green pepper.
3. Boil the provisions until tender, but not crushed.
4. Test by sticking with a fork.
5. Serve with white rice, rice & peas and the mountain chicken.

No. 35 RED PEA SOUP

Most likely to be found: All over the Caribbean.
Alternative Names: Pea Soup, Saturday Soup.

THE SECRET: Caribbean Saturday soups are a meal within themselves, as they are packed with meat and vegetables (Ground Provisions/Hard Food). The secret to a perfect Caribbean soup is to ensure that the vegetables do not disintegrate during cooking. This can be achieved by having all of your meat, vegetables and dumplings fully prepared so that there is little delay in adding them to your Dutch Pot/stock pot.

OTHER BACKGROUND INFORMATION: Despite the name Red Pea soup is *not* a vegetarian dish. To change Red Pea Soup to Beef Soup all you need to do is to replace the salted meat with 450 g/1 lb of diced stewing steak at Step 3 opposite.

INGREDIENTS (SERVES 8–10):
2 x 400 g tins/cans of red peas/kidney beans (or 450 g/1 lb
    dried red peas/kidney beans, soaked overnight)
3 cups/720 ml/24 fl oz water, for soaking peas (to be
    discarded)
450 g/1 lb salt beef/salted pig's tails/stewing steak, diced
2 litres/4 pints of water, for soup
2 cups/480 ml/16 fl oz meat/vegetable stock, for soup
3 cloves of garlic, chopped
3 sprigs of thyme, chopped
225 g/½ lb yellow yam
225 g/½ lb white yam
225 g/½ lb chocho
225 g/½ lb dasheen
225 g/½ lb sweet potatoes
1 tsp oil, for browning meat
3 escallions or medium onions
2 Scotch bonnet, whole
15–20 dumplings/spinners (See: Recipe No. 30)
½ tsp black pepper (optional)
1 x 400 ml tin/can coconut milk

METHOD:

1. a) Dried peas/beans must be washed and soaked in cold water overnight prior to use (removing any damaged peas). Discard water from the peas and follow Step3a for the cooking method.
   b) If using tinned peas, follow Step 3b for the cooking method.
2. a) If using salted meat soak overnight in cold water, changing the water 3–4 times before use. Remove the water from the salted meat and cut into small pieces and set aside.
3. If using stewing steak, no pre-soaking is required. However, the meat still needs to be diced and set aside.
   a) Add the rehydrated peas, fresh water, stock, garlic and thyme to a Dutch Pot/heavy-bottomed pan. Bring to the boil, reduce the heat, cover and simmer for 1½ hours; OR
   b) Add the tinned peas, water, stock, garlic and thyme to the pot. Bring to the boil, reduce the heat and simmer for 30 minutes.
4. Peel, wash and cut into equal sized cubes the yam, chocho, dasheen and sweet potatoes. Place in a bowl of cold water until ready to use.
5. Heat the oil in a frying pan, brown the diced meat, add to the pot and stir, then add the root vegetables and stir.
6. Roughly chop the escallions/onions. Add to the pot and stir.
7. Add the whole Scotch bonnet peppers to the soup (**NB** – The Scotch bonnet/chilli peppers are used whole for flavouring only and should be removed prior to serving.)
8. Stir the soup and then cook for 35–45 minutes until the meat, peas and vegetables are tender.
9. Make the dough for the dumplings/spinners (see: Recipe No. 30) and set aside.
10. Using a fork or spoon remove a single piece of meat, peas and root vegetable from the soup. Taste to check that all the key ingredients are cooked.
11. Once the main ingredients are cooked, add the dumplings/spinners to the soup, stir and cook for a further 10 minutes.
12. Add the black pepper (optional) and coconut milk to the soup and stir.
13. Remove the whole Scotch bonnet peppers from the soup prior to serving and discard. Serve.

No. 36 CREAM OF CALLALOO SOUP

Most likely to be found: All over the Caribbean.
Alternative Name: Callaloo Soup.

THE SECRET: Fresh callaloo is the secret of an authentic dish, but if this is not available you can use the tinned/canned variety. Alternatively, you can buy some callaloo seeds and grow your own. As with most Caribbean soups a hot pepper, such as whole Scotch bonnet pepper, is added to the dish for flavour, but removed prior to serving.

OTHER BACKGROUND INFORMATION: If you are concerned about losing your Scotch bonnet pepper in the dish during the cooking process you can tie a piece of string to the stem and then tie the other end to the pan/pot handle or lid, to make it easier to retrieve later.

INGREDIENTS (SERVES 6):
450 g/1 lb fresh callaloo or 1 x 400 g–500 g tin/can callaloo
2 escallion stalks or 1 small onion, diced
1 litre/2 pints vegetable stock (vegetable bouillon)
1 or 2 whole Scotch bonnet/chilli peppers
½ cup/120 ml/4 fl oz coconut milk
¼ tsp black pepper
¼ tsp salt (to taste)

METHOD:

1. Wash and chop the fresh callaloo, escallion/onion. (If using tinned callaloo there is no need to wash.)
2. Add the stock, vegetables and whole chilli pepper(s)to a Dutch Pot/heavy-bottomed pan and bring to the boil. (**NB:** The Scotch bonnet/chilli pepper is used whole for flavouring only and should be removed prior to serving.)
3. Reduce the heat and simmer until the vegetables are cooked.
4. Remove the pot from the heat.
5. Remove the whole pepper from the soup and discard.
6. Allow the other ingredients to cool.
7. Purée the mixture in a food processor and then return to the heat.
8. Add the coconut milk, and salt and pepper to taste.
9. Simmer for a few minutes and serve hot.
10. Serve with hard dough bread.

No. 37 CORN SOUP

Most likely to be found in: Trinidad & Tobago.

THE SECRET: Corn Soup is served with plenty of pepper sauce. If you are making this soup for non-vegetarians, you can replace the vegetable stock with a meat stock. Smoked ham bones (available from any good butcher) can be used to make a great stock, which will add a deep smoky flavour to your soup.

OTHER BACKGROUND INFORMATION: Corn Soup is very popular with revellers at carnival time in Trinidad & Tobago where it is eaten with lots of hot pepper sauce.

INGREDIENTS (SERVES 6–10):

2 tbsp vegetable oil
2 onions, finely chopped
3 cloves of garlic, finely diced
450 g/1 lb potatoes, peeled and quartered
2 carrots, diced
¼ cup celery, finely chopped
⅓ cup chopped fresh thyme
½ tsp allspice (pimenta/pimento berries), ground
¾ cup yellow split peas
8 cups/1.9 litres/64 fl oz vegetable/meat stock
salt and black pepper (to taste)
1 hot (Scotch bonnet) pepper, left whole
½ cup/120 ml/4 fl oz coconut milk (optional)
15–20 boiled dumplings/spinners (see: Recipe No. 30)
6 ears of corn, cut into 5 cm/2 inch pieces
¼ cup Chadon Beni (Thai Parsley or fresh coriander/cilantro) chopped
⅓ cup chives, chopped

METHOD:
1. In a large Dutch Pot or stock pot heat the oil.
2. Add the onions and garlic and sauté until fragrant.
3. Add the potatoes, carrots, celery, thyme and ground allspice and cook for about 5 minutes, stirring constantly.
4. Add the split peas and stock.
5. Add salt and black pepper to taste.
6. Add the whole Scotch bonnet pepper and coconut milk (optional).
7. Cover the pot and simmer for about an hour until the peas are soft.
8. Use a stick/immersion or ordinary blender and purée the soup to a thick and creamy consistency and return to the pot.
9. Make the dumplings/spinners (see: Recipe No. 30).
10. Add the corn and dumplings and cook for a further 20 minutes until the corn is cooked and the dumplings float to the surface.
11. Add the Chadon Beni, remove from the heat, taste and adjust the seasonings.
12. If the soup is too thick at any time, add water.
13. Garnish with a sprinkle of chopped chives (optional) and serve.

No. 38 MONK'S BLACK BEANS (SOUP)

(NATIONAL DISH: CUBA)

Most likely to be found in: Cuba.
Alternative Name: Black Bean Soup.

THE SECRET: Do not season black beans until they are fully cooked, otherwise they may become tough.

OTHER BACKGROUND INFORMATION: In local Cuban restaurants, chefs often create a *Cuban Sandwich* (aka *Cubano*) which is served along with the *Monk's Black Bean*. The Cuban Sandwich is made from a long thin loaf of hard crust Cuban bread (or French stick) stacked high with thin slices of roast pork, ham, Swiss cheese, Serrano ham, dill pickles and yellow mustard (or mayonnaise) and then toasted.

INGREDIENTS (SERVES 6):
2 x 400 g tins/cans black beans or 240 g/8 oz dry/drained
    weight) or 2 cups dried black beans (soaked overnight)
1 large onion, finely diced
1 green pepper, finely diced
2 tsp oregano
4 cloves of garlic, crushed
3 tbsp olive oil
2 pimiento peppers, minced
3 tsp salt
2 tbsp ground black pepper
1 bay leaf
3 tsp sugar
3 tsp vinegar
3 tsp cooking wine
2 tbsp olive oil

METHOD:

1. If using dried black beans, soak them overnight in enough water to cover the beans.
2. Cook the dried beans in a thick-bottomed pan for at least 1 hour or until they become tender (topping up with water as necessary).
3. In a frying pan, fry the finely minced onion, pepper, oregano and garlic in oil.
4. Drain the water off the beans.
5. Pour about one can/cup of the beans in the pan and crush them well (or use a food processor to purée the beans).
6. Add in this mixture, as well as the minced pimiento peppers, to a Dutch Pot with the remaining beans. Add the salt, pepper, bay leaf, sugar and water to cover and then bring to a boil.
7. Cover the pot and simmer for about 1 hour.
8. Add the vinegar, cooking wine and simmer for another 60–90 minutes.
9. If you find that the soup is too runny, uncover the pot and simmer for a little longer.
10. Prior to serving stir in 2 tbsp of oil.
11. Serve with Cuba Sandwich or white rice.

No. 39 CARIBBEAN CHICKEN NOODLE SOUP

Most likely to be found in: Jamaica.
Alternative Name: Saturday Soup.

THE SECRET: The key to this dish is to ensure that the vegetables do not overcook and fall apart. Timing is everything. Using a good chicken stock greatly enhances the flavour. The Scotch bonnet peppers are used whole so that you get some of the pepper's flavour without overpowering the other ingredients.

OTHER BACKGROUND INFORMATION: This is a very hearty soup that is a complete meal by itself. This dish must be served hot and can be used for lunch or evening meal.

INGREDIENTS (SERVES 8–10):
450 g/1 lb fresh chicken wings (cut through joints)
3 tbsp vinegar (for washing chicken)
225 g/½ lb cho–cho, chopped into 2.5 cm/1 inch cubes
225 g/½ lb pumpkin or butternut squash, chopped into
    2.5 cm/1 inch cubes
225 g/½ lb yam, chopped into 2.5 cm/1 inch cubes
225 g/½ lb carrots, chopped
225 g/½ lb dasheen, chopped into 2.5 cm/1 inch cubes
225 g/½ lb cassava, chopped into 2.5 cm/1 inch cubes
1 tbsp oil
1 medium onion, fine dice
2 escallion pieces, chopped
1 clove of garlic, crushed
2 tsp ground black pepper
Sprig of fresh thyme, chopped
1 litre/2 pints chicken stock/bouillon
560 ml/1 pint water
1 pack chicken noodle soup
2 Scotch bonnet peppers, whole
20–30 dumplings/spinners (see: Recipe No. 30)
1 x 400 ml tin/can coconut milk

METHOD:
Prepare Chicken:
1. Prepare the chicken wings using the vinegar (optional). (See: *Meat and Fish Preparation – Caribbean Style*, page 9.)

Prepare Vegetables:
1. Peel and dice all the vegetables (to a similar size, but not too small) and add to a large bowl of water to prevent them going brown prior to cooking. (**NB** If the vegetables are cut too small they will fall apart during the cooking process.)

Brown Chicken Wings:
1. Heat a large Dutch Pot/stock pot on high heat and add the oil.
2. Add the chicken wings and brown quickly on high heat for 5 minutes and then remove from the pot (leaving the oil in the pot) and set aside.

Prepare Soup:
1. Add the onion, escallions, garlic, black pepper and thyme to the pot and stir.
2. Drain the water from the vegetables and add them to the pot and stir.
3. Add the chicken stock to the pot and enough water to cover the vegetables, and stir.
4. Add the chicken noodle soup mix pack/packet to the pot, stir and bring to the boil.
5. Reduce the heat so that the soup is simmering and add the whole Scotch bonnet peppers.
6. While the soup/vegetables are cooking, prepare the dough for the dumplings/spinners (see: Recipe No. 30) and set aside for 20 minutes.
7. After 30 minutes use a fork to test whether the vegetables are cooked (the fork should comfortably go into the vegetables without them falling apart).
8. Once the vegetables are cooked add the browned chicken wings to the soup and stir.
9. Use the dough to make the dumplings/spinners and add them directly to the pot and stir.
10. Add the coconut milk to the pot, stir and bring back to simmer for a further 10–15 minutes to allow the dumpling/spinners to cook.

11. If the soup is too runny, mix 2 teaspoons of corn starch/cornflour with 2 teaspoons of cold water and gradually add to the soup, stirring constantly.
12. Remove the soup from the heat.
13. Remove the whole Scotch bonnet peppers from the soup and discard.
14. Wait approximately 15 minutes prior to serving as the soup will be very hot (especially if cooked in a Dutch Pot).
15. Serve.

No. 40 PUERTO RICAN PORK WITH SPANISH RICE & PIGEON PEAS

(NATIONAL DISH: PUERTO RICO)

Most likely to be found in: Puerto Rico, Anguilla.
Alternative Names: Arroz con Gandules and Pernil; Rice and Pigeon Peas, with Roasted Pork Shoulder.

THE SECRET: A good *Sofrito* (base cooking sauce) is the secret of this great dish. It is made by combination of crushed garlic, diced onions, sweet peppers and tomatoes which are slowly sautéed or braised in olive oil until the main ingredients form a smooth thick sauce. *Alcaparrado* is a Puerto Rican Olive & Pepper Mix, which helps to give this dish a distinct flavour.

OTHER BACKGROUND INFORMATION: The crispy rice that sticks to the bottom of the pot is called 'pegao' and is highly sought after by Puerto Ricans.

INGREDIENTS (SERVES 6–8):
For Sofrito (Base Cooking Sauce):
1 tsp olive oil
1 medium white onion, chopped finely
1 green bell pepper, chopped finely
4 cloves of garlic, minced
1 x 400g can/tin chopped tomatoes

For Spanish Rice and Pigeon Peas:
3 tbsp oil
2 tbsp Alcaparrado (capers and olives mixture)
1 portion of Sofrito
1 portion of Sazon Con Achiote (seasoned salt/chicken stock cube), optional
1 x 400 g can/tin pigeon peas (brown/green variety) – including water
2 cups/400 g/14 oz long grain rice
2 cups/480 ml/16 fl oz chicken stock
1 tsp ground cumin (geera)
½ tsp fresh/dry coriander (cilantro)
½ tsp fresh/dry oregano
½ tsp salt (to taste)
½ tsp pepper (to taste)

For Roast Pork Marinade:
6 cloves of garlic, crushed
1 tsp salt
½ tsp black pepper
½ tsp oregano, finely chopped
1 meat stock cube (optional)
2 tbsp olive oil
2.25 kg/5 lb pork picnic shoulder*
3 tsp vinegar/lime juice (optional)

(*pork picnic shoulder = pork arm shoulder. This comes from the lower
part of the pig's shoulder.)

METHOD:
Prepare Sofrito (Base Cooking Sauce):
1. Heat the oil in a frying pan.
2. Add the onion and green pepper, then sauté until soft.
3. Add the garlic, chopped tomatoes, and cook for 20–30 minutes on
   medium heat until the sauce is reduced by 25 per cent.
4. Remove the sauce from the heat and set aside.

Arroz con Gandules Preparation:
1. Add the oil, Alcaparrado, Sofrito and Sazon to a pre-heated medium
   sized pan, and cook over medium heat for 4–5 minutes.
2. Add the pigeon peas and all the other ingredients (except the salt and
   pepper), plus enough water to cover the rice by the level of 2.5 cm/1
   inch.
3. Add salt and pepper to taste and bring to the boil.
4. Reduce the heat, stir gently with a fork, cover the pan and cook for
   30 minutes on low heat (or until the rice is cooked).

Pork Preparation:
Note: The meat should be marinade pork, refrigerated for at least **24
hours** before cooking, as in the following Steps 1–8:
1. In a small bowl mix together the crushed garlic, salt, pepper, oregano,
   stock cube and olive oil.
2. Prepare the pork using vinegar/lime juice (optional). (See: *Meat and
   Fish Preparation – Caribbean Style*, page 9.)
3. Remove the excess liquid.

4. Using a sharp knife, remove the fat and skin from the pork shoulder meat, trying to keep it all in one piece, starting at the wide end of the meat and moving towards the narrow end.
5. Season the meat and then replace the pork fat and skin (use oven-proof string to tie on the skin and fat, if necessary).
6. Rub some salt into the skin of the meat.
7. Make very deep slits all over the skin of the meat (avoiding the string) and ensure that the seasoning goes into all the slits.
8. Place the meat in a large bowl, cover and refrigerate for 24 hours.

The Next Day:
1. Remove the meat from the refrigerator and allow to stand for at least 1 hour to let the meat get back to room temperature before cooking.
2. Place the meat in a deep roasting pan (fat side up), uncovered.
3. Preheat the oven to 400°F/200°C/Gas Mark 6 for at least 30 minutes before placing the meat inside.
4. Cook in the hot oven for 1 hour, and then reduce the heat to 350°F/180°C/Gas Mark 4 for a further 4–5 hours until the meat is very tender and coming off the bone. (**NB:** The pork should be cooked when there is no pink meat and the juices run clear and the core temperature is between 75°C and 85°C.)
5. When the meat is done, you can prick it on the side with a fork to see if it shreds.
6. If the pork skin (crackling) is not crispy you can raise the temperature back to 400°F/200°C/Gas Mark 6 for 15–20 minutes.
7. Remove the meat from the oven, remove the string and allow the meat to rest for at least 30–45 minutes before serving.
8. Remove the crackling (skin) prior to carving.
9. Serve with rice.

No. 41 JERK PORK

Most likely to be found in: Jamaica.

THE SECRET: Jerk Rub Jamaica, authentic Jerk meats and fish are smoked/cooked slowly over a low heat on a pimenta wood barbecue. Why not try this recipe using a pork shoulder or leg joint instead of pork loin pieces? These joints will take several hours to cook on a low heat, but the results are amazing.

OTHER BACKGROUND INFORMATION: Genuine Jerk meats (or fish) are barbecued/smoked with pimenta leaves or with pimenta wood (not widely available) being added to the barbecue coals, which also adds to the authentic taste. Oak wood chips can be used as a substitute for pimenta leaves or wood.

INGREDIENTS (SERVES 6):
8 pieces (1.3 kg/3 lb) boneless pork loin
2 tbsp white vinegar (optional)
2 tsp lime (optional)
3 tsp Jerk Rub (for marinade – see: Recipe No. 51)
2 tbsp oil
250 ml/9 fl oz Jerk Marinade (for basting – see: Recipe No. 52)
1 portion (50 ml/2 fl oz) Jerk Dipping Sauce (to serve) – see: Recipe No. 53

METHOD:

1. Prepare the pork using the vinegar/lime juice (optional). (See: *Meat and Fish Preparation – Caribbean Style*, page 9.)
2. Remove the excess liquid.
3. With a sharp knife trim off any excess fat, skin or sinew.
4. Place the pork pieces, Jerk Rub and oil in a bowl, and using disposable gloves work the Jerk Rub into the pork.
5. Cover the bowl and marinade the pork in the refrigerator for at least 6 hours (or preferably overnight).
6. Take the marinated pork out of the refrigerator 30 minutes prior to grilling.
7. Wrap each piece of pork in kitchen foil and grill on a preheated barbecue or grill on low heat (top rack of barbecue or middle rack of grill oven) for 30 minutes.
8. After 30 minutes remove the pork from the foil and place on a rack nearer to the heat for a further 15 minutes (turning every 3–4 minutes and basting with the Jerk Marinade).
9. Once the pork is cooked, allow to rest for 10 minutes prior to serving.
10. Serve with rice and peas, salad and Jerk Dipping Sauce.

No. 42 FISH TEA (SOUP)

Most likely to be found in: Jamaica.
Alternative Name: Fish Soup.

THE SECRET: Fish Tea should never be boiled during the cooking process, as this will lead to impurities from the fish affecting the taste and texture of the broth.

OTHER BACKGROUND INFORMATION: Unlike most other Caribbean soups, Fish Tea is in the strictest sense a light soup/broth.

INGREDIENTS (SERVES 6):
900 g/2 lb small fish
2 tbsp white vinegar (optional)
1 lime or 2 tsp lime juice (optional)
3 escallion/green onions stalks, medium diced
1 sprig of thyme
2 large or medium cloves of garlic
12 cups/2.8 litres/96 fl oz water
2 medium potatoes, peeled and cut into small pieces – leave in water to prevent them going brown
salt and black pepper (to taste)
4 fingers of green bananas (do not peel or cut until ready for use)
1 Scotch bonnet pepper, whole
6 pimenta seeds/berries, whole

METHOD:

1. Prepare the fish using the vinegar/lime juice (optional). (See: *Meat and Fish Preparation – Caribbean Style*, page 9.)
2. Remove the excess liquid.
3. With a sharp knife trim off any excess fat, skin or sinew.
4. Add the fish, escallion, thyme, and garlic to a warm Dutch Pot/stock pot.
5. Add the water and bring to the boil.
6. Reduce the heat immediately and simmer the ingredients until the fish comes off the bone.
7. Pour the contents through a strainer and remove all the bones.
8. Add the potatoes and salt to the strained soup.
9. Peel the green bananas and add to the soup.
10. Let the soup simmer, then add the thyme, escallion, pepper, pimenta and black pepper.
11. Simmer for another 10 minutes and then serve.

No. 43 FISH & FUNGI

(NATIONAL DISH: US AND BRITISH VIRGIN ISLANDS)

Most likely to be found in: The US Virgin Islands
and British Virgin Islands.
Alternative Name: Boiled Fish and Okra Fungi.

THE SECRET: The secret of good fungi is to stir it vigorously during the cooking process, so that you end up with a very smooth mixture that is not coarse or lumpy. The addition of okra is optional.

OTHER BACKGROUND INFORMATION: Fungi (pronounced foon-ji) can be described simply as a stiff cornmeal mush.

INGREDIENTS (SERVES 6):
For Fish Style Fish:
2 kg/4½ lb fish, scaled and gutted
1 medium tomato, chopped
2 medium onions, chopped
3 tbsp lime or lemon juice
1 tbsp malt vinegar
2 tsp butter
2 cups/480 ml/16 fl oz water

Okra Fungi
10 oz fresh chopped okra
2½ cups/600 ml/1 pint water
1½ cups cornmeal flour (fine)
2 tbsp butter
salt and pepper (to taste)

METHOD:

Prepare Fish:

1. Season the fish with the chopped tomato, onion, lime or lemon juice, vinegar and leave to marinade for about 30 minutes.
2. Add the butter and water to a saucepan and heat.
3. Add the fish and marinade to the saucepan and cook the fish on medium to low heat for approximately 20 minutes, until the flesh of the fish is nicely cooked (but not falling off the bone).
4. Remove from the heat and allow to stand prior to serving.
5. Serve the fish with the tomato sauce in which it was cooked.

Prepare Fungi:

1. Cook the okra in boiling water until tender (approximately 5–6 minutes).
2. In a medium size saucepan, bring the water to a boil.
3. In order to reduce the possibility of a lumpy fungi it is suggested that you mix about ¼ cup of the cornmeal with ¾ cup of water in a separate small bowl.
4. Add the mixture back into the larger pot of boiling water.
5. Let the cornmeal cook for about a minute, then add the rest of the cornmeal into the pan in a slow steady stream, while stirring constantly.
6. Add the hot cooked okra to the cooked cornmeal. Stir well.
7. Then, stir in the butter, salt and pepper, to taste.
8. Simmer for about 5 minutes more.

No. 44 BULLY BEEF & RICE

Most likely to be found in: Jamaica, Trinidad & Tobago.
Alternative Names: Spiced Corn Beef & Rice, Corned Beef & Rice.

THE SECRET: This dish is all about the sauce. The combination of onions, tomatoes, garlic, paprika, thyme and black pepper in the right proportions can turn a plain tin/can of corned beef into something mouth-watering.

OTHER BACKGROUND INFORMATION: The appearance of this dish can be ruined if corned beef pieces fall apart during the cooking process, so do not stir into the dish too vigorously once the corned beef is added; and store opened corned beef in the refrigerator for 30 minutes prior to cutting into small cubes and cooking.

INGREDIENTS (SERVES 6):
1 tbsp vegetable oil or coconut oil
1 medium onion or 2 escallion stalks, chopped
1 clove of garlic, crushed (optional)
1 tsp paprika
2 sprigs of fresh thyme
1 Scotch bonnet pepper, deseeded and chopped or 2 tsp
    pepper sauce (optional)
2 tomatoes, chopped
3 tbsp tomato ketchup/tomato purée
1 can corned beef (fridge temperature), chopped into cubes
1 tsp black ground pepper

METHOD:

1. Heat the oil in a heavy-bottomed frying pan over moderate heat.
2. Add the chopped onion/escallions, and sauté until the onions are golden brown (but not burnt).
3. Add the garlic, paprika, thyme and Scotch bonnet pepper (optional).
4. Add the chopped tomatoes, stir well and cook for 10–15 minutes until the tomatoes are broken down.
5. Add the tomato ketchup/purée.
6. Fold the corned beef cubes into the sauce, until covered. (Do not stir to avoid the cubes becoming crushed.)
7. Use a teaspoon to remove any excess oil from the top of the dish.
8. Sprinkle black pepper on top, and then serve when piping hot.
9. Bully Beef is usually served for breakfast with Johnny Cakes (fried or boiled dumplings), boiled green bananas or toast. It can also be served with white rice and plantain.

No. 45 ROASTED BREADFRUIT & FRIED JACKFISH

(NATIONAL DISH: ST VINCENT & THE GRENADINES)

Most likely to be found in: St Vincent & the Grenadines.

THE SECRET: This is a reasonably straightforward dish which can only be spoilt by over frying the fish.

OTHER BACKGROUND INFORMATION: This dish can be served for breakfast, lunch or dinner.

INGREDIENTS (SERVES 6):
1 large breadfruit
450 g/1 lb jackfish
3 tbsp lime/lemon juice
¼ cup minced seasoning (onion, chive, garlic, thyme)
1 tbsp salt
1 cup flour for coating (add as desired)
oil (for frying)

For Sauce Preparation (Optional):
1 tbsp oil (for frying)
1 medium onion, minced
1 clove of garlic, minced
1 sprig of thyme
1 medium ripe tomato, sliced
15 g/½ oz margarine
1 tsp tomato paste or ketchup
1 cup/240 ml/8 fl oz water
salt and pepper (to taste)
1 small sweet pepper (for garnish)

METHOD:
Roast Breadfruit:
1. **Warning:** Pierce the breadfruit with a fork or skewer, before placing it in the oven for roasting (failure to do this could result in an explosion of the breadfruit causing possible damage to the oven and/or personal injury from the fruit's internal pressure).
2. Remove the stalk from the breadfruit and then roast/bake in a moderate oven at 350°F/180°C/Gas Mark 4 for about 1½–2 hours or until soft.
3. Slice the breadfruit in half, and then divide each half into two or three pieces to produce 1cm/½ inch slices, peeling away the skin and core.

Preparing & Cooking the Fried Jackfish:
1. Clean and prepare the fish using the lime juice (optional). See page 9.
2. Pour the lime/lemon juice over the jackfish.
3. Leave to marinate for 15 minutes.
4. Rinse the jackfish and dry with paper towels.
5. Add salt to the minced seasoning.
6. Rub the seasoning over the fish and set aside.
7. Sprinkle some flour on greaseproof/wax paper.
8. Coat the fish on both sides in the flour – remove the excess.
9. Heat the oil in a frying pan on medium heat until very hot but not smoking.
10. Fry the fish for approximately 4 minutes on each side or until brown.
11. Serve with the sliced breadfruit.

Sauce Preparation (Optional):
1. Heat the oil in a pan, then sauté the onion, garlic, thyme and sliced tomato in it until softened.
2. Add the margarine and stir until melted.
3. Add the tomato paste or ketchup and water.
4. Add salt and pepper to taste.
5. Simmer until slightly thickened.
6. Remove from the heat, cool, garnish with the sweet pepper, and serve with the breadfruit and jackfish.

No. 46 PICADILLO

(NATIONAL DISH: CUBA)

Most likely to be found in: Cuba.

THE SECRET: The secret of any good Cuban dish is the '*sofrito*' (base cooking sauce) which is a combination of crushed garlic, diced onions and sweet peppers and tomatoes which are slowly sautéed or braised in olive oil until the main ingredients form a smooth thick sauce.

OTHER BACKGROUND INFORMATION: It has been very difficult during our research to establish a single Cuban national dish, but this is definitely a Cuban favourite.

INGREDIENTS (SERVES 6–8):
For Sofrito (base cooking sauce):
1 tsp olive oil
1 medium white onion, chopped finely
1 green bell pepper, chopped finely
4 cloves of garlic, minced
¾ cup/180 ml/6 fl oz tomato sauce
½ cup/120 ml/4 fl oz water
½ cup/120 ml/4 fl oz beef stock

For Picadillo:
900 g/2 lb ground beef/mince
1 tsp oregano
1 tsp cumin (geera)
salt and pepper (to taste)
1 tsp olive oil, for browning beef
1 portion of Sofrito (base cooking sauce)
8–10 green olives, pitted and chopped
½ cup raisins
2 bay leaves (optional)
2 small potatoes, peeled and diced

METHOD:

Prepare Sofrito (base cooking sauce):
1. Heat the oil in a frying pan.
2. Add the onion and green pepper, then sauté until soft.
3. Add the garlic, tomato sauce, water and stock, and cook for 20–30 minutes on medium heat until the sauce is reduced by 25 per cent.
4. Remove the sauce from the heat and set aside.

Prepare Picadillo:
1. In a mixing bowl, combine the ground beef, oregano, cumin, salt and pepper.
2. In a clean frying pan heat the oil and then add the beef to brown.
3. Add the sofrito (sauce) olives, raisins and bay leaves to the mixture.
4. Cover the pan and cook over medium-low heat for 15 minutes.
5. Add the diced potato to the pan.
6. Cover and cook for another 15 minutes, or until the potatoes are done.
7. Remove the cover and cook, uncovered, for a further 10 minutes or until the liquid is fully evaporated (however, the meat should still be moist at the end of cooking).
8. Skim off any oil/fat sitting on top of the dish prior to serving.
9. Allow the dish to stand for 10–15 minutes before serving.
10. Serve the traditional Cuban way with Cuban (stewed) black beans, white rice and fried plantain.

No. 47 ROPA VIEJA
(NATIONAL DISH: CUBA)

Most likely to be found in: Cuba.
Alternative Name: Shredded Beef in Tomato Sauce.

THE SECRET: Do not try to rush the cooking of this dish. The slower the better (within reason). The secret of any good Cuban dish is the '*sofrito*' (base cooking sauce) which is a combination of crushed garlic, diced onions and sweet peppers and tomatoes which are slowly sautéed or braised in olive oil until the main ingredients form a smooth thick sauce.

OTHER BACKGROUND INFORMATION: A *flank steak* (aka bavette), is a beef steak cut from the abdominal muscles of the cow.

INGREDIENTS (SERVES 6):
For Sofrito (base cooking sauce):
1 tsp olive oil
1 large onion, diced
1 green pepper, deseeded and cut into 2.5 cm/1 inch squares
1 red pepper, deseeded and cut into 2.5 cm/1 inch squares
6 cloves of garlic, crushed
3 fresh medium tomatoes, chopped
1 cup/240 ml/8 fl oz beef stock/broth
1 x 8 oz (small) tin of tomato purée
1 tbsp white vinegar

For Ropa Vieja:
1 tbsp vegetable oil
900 g/2 lb beef flank steak (bavette)
2 tsp ground cumin (geera)
1 tsp chopped fresh coriander (cilantro)
1 jar of black olives, chopped (optional)
2 tsp dried raisins (optional)
1 tsp salt (to taste)

METHOD:
Prepare Sofrito (Base Cooking Sauce):
1. Heat the oil in a frying pan.
2. Add the onion and peppers, then sauté until soft.
3. Add the garlic, tomatoes, stock, tomato purée and vinegar and cook for 20–30 minutes on medium heat until the sauce is reduced by 25 per cent.
4. Remove the sauce from the heat and set aside.

Prepare Ropa Vieja:
1. Heat the vegetable oil in a Dutch Pot or large frying pan over medium-high heat.
2. Brown the flank steak on each side, about 4–5 minutes per side.
3. Transfer the beef to a slow cooker (or keep in the Dutch Pot but reduce heat to its lowest setting).
4. Pour in the Sofrito (sauce) and stir until well blended.
5. Add the cumin, coriander, olives, raisins and salt to taste to the pot and stir.
6. Cover and slow cook on a very low heat for 5–8 hours, until the beef can be shredded easily with a fork. (**NB:** The cooking time can be speeded up by using a pressure cooker, but you may lose some of the flavour.)
7. When ready to serve, shred the meat.
8. Serve the traditional Cuban way with Cuban (stewed) black beans, white rice and fried plantain.

No. 48 PORC-COLOMBO
(National Dish: Guadeloupe)

Most likely to be found in: Guadeloupe.
Alternative Names: Pork Colombo, Caribbean Pork Curry,
Creole Pork Curry.

THE SECRET: For authentic Porc-Colombo, you need to use *Colombo Powder*, a French, West Indian curry powder, which can be purchased online or in specialist ethnic food stores and markets.

OTHER BACKGROUND INFORMATION: If you are unable to locate Colombo Powder easily you can try making your own (see: Recipe No. 55).

INGREDIENTS (SERVES 6):
800 g/1¾ lb pork loin (known locally as porc)
7 cloves of garlic
salt, pepper, vinegar
2 chillies (1 chopped and 1 whole)
1 pinch of clove powder
4 chives
5 parsley sprigs
1 onion
1 tsp oil (for frying)
1 pinch of coriander and aniseed
1 sprig of thyme, chopped
1 green mango, chopped
1 aubergine
1 courgette (zucchini)
3 medium potatoes, peeled
2 heaped tsp Colombo Powder or curry powder
    (garam masala)
juice of 1 lemon

METHOD:

1. Cut the meat into pieces. Chop **5** of the garlic cloves, then season the meat with the salt, pepper, the 5 chopped garlic cloves, **1** chopped chilli, the clove powder and a little vinegar.

2. Allow the meat to marinate in the seasoning for approximately 30 minutes in the refrigerator.

3. Chop finely the chives, parsley, onion and the rest of the garlic, and then fry them gently in a teaspoon of oil in a Dutch Pot. Add the coriander, aniseed and thyme to the pot.

4. Add the meat and the chopped mango and let the meat brown.

5. Add the second chilli to the pot.

6. Chop the aubergine, courgette and the peeled potatoes.

7. Add the chopped vegetables to the meat in the pot together with the Colombo Powder (or curry powder).

8. Add water to the pot so that it covers the meat, stir, put the lid on the pot and simmer for about 50 minutes (stirring occasionally).

9. Taste, and correct the seasoning with salt and pepper as necessary.

10. Add the lemon juice a few minutes before the end of cooking, and then serve.

No. 49 CARIBBEAN VEGETABLE CURRY

Most likely to be found: All over the Caribbean.
Alternative Names: Curry Vegetables, Curried Vegetables.

THE SECRET: ★The amount of curry powder used varies from island to island. For example, a Jamaican cook may only use 2 tablespoons of curry powder and add black pepper. Whereas an eastern Caribbean cook may use more curry powder (3–4 tablespoons) and no black pepper.

OTHER BACKGROUND INFORMATION: Larger Ground Provision vegetables such as yams, chocho, sweet potatoes, etc may also be used subject to seasonal availability.

INGREDIENTS (SERVES 6):
4 tbsp vegetable oil
1 small onion, diced
2.5 cm/1 inch piece of fresh ginger, grated
2 tsp Caribbean curry powder (to taste)
2 tsp black pepper (optional)
1 tbsp minced garlic
2 carrots, diced
2 potatoes, diced
450 g/1 lb green beans, stems removed
1 x 450 g/16 oz tin/can chickpeas, drained and rinsed
2 cups/480 ml/16 fl oz vegetable stock
225 g/8 oz pumpkin or butternut squash
1 cup/240 ml/8 fl oz coconut milk

METHOD:

1. Heat the oil in a Dutch Pot/thick-bottomed pan on medium heat.
2. Add the onion and ginger, and cook for 2 minutes.
3. Add the curry powder and black pepper, and cook for a further 2 minutes.
4. Reduce the heat and add the garlic, carrots and potatoes, stirring occasionally for 7–10 minutes.
5. Add the green beans, chickpeas and half the stock.
6. Stir occasionally for 5–7 minutes.
7. Add the rest of the stock.
8. Add the pumpkin/butternut squash.
9. Stir, cover and allow to cook for 7–10 minutes.
10. Reduce the heat to simmer.
11. Add the coconut milk and cook for a further 2–3 minutes.
12. Cover and cook until all the vegetables are just softened, stirring occasionally – about 20 minutes.

No. 50 CARIBBEAN
HOT PEPPER SAUCE

Most likely to be found: All over the Caribbean.
Alternative Names: Hot Sauce, Pepper Sauce.

THE SECRET: This is one recipe where you are free to experiment to your heart's content, as the combination of ingredients differs widely.

OTHER BACKGROUND INFORMATION: While there are more Caribbean hot pepper sauces on the market than there are islands within the entire Caribbean, this should not stop you from trying to make your own with its own special twist.

INGREDIENTS (SERVES 6):
1 tbsp vegetable oil
10 small hot peppers (Scotch bonnet, habanero chilli or any
      other variety you can get your hands on), chopped
2 medium carrots, roughly diced
2 medium onions, roughly diced
4 cloves of garlic, whole
1 cm/½ inch of ginger, roughly diced
10 pimenta (allspice) berries, ground
1 tbsp brown sugar
3 tsp salt
½ tsp turmeric, ground
½ tsp cumin (geera)
3 tsp arrowroot (to thicken)
1 cup/240 ml/8 fl oz white vinegar
½ cup/120 ml/4 fl oz white wine vinegar (optional)

METHOD:

1. Heat the oil in a roasting tray.
2. Add the chopped peppers, carrots, onions, garlic and ginger and roast for 30 minutes on medium heat until the vegetables are slightly caramelized (but not burnt).
3. Place the roasted ingredients in a saucepan and add the allspice, sugar, salt, turmeric, cumin, arrowroot and 1 cup of white vinegar.
4. Stir and bring the ingredients to the boil.
5. Reduce the heat and then simmer on low heat for 30 minutes
6. Remove the pan from the heat and allow the ingredients to cool for 15 minutes.
7. Pour the cooled ingredients into a blender and blend into a smooth paste.
8. If you want to dilute your pepper sauce to a thinner consistency, heat some white wine vinegar in a saucepan and stir into your sauce a little bit at a time until you have a thinner, smoother sauce.
9. Once the pepper sauce is almost cool, but not cold, transfer into a glass jar and store in the fridge.

No. 51 JERK RUB

(DRY SEASONING)

Most likely to be found in: Jamaica.
Alternative Names: Jerk Seasoning, Dry Jerk Rub.

THE SECRET: Dry rub is best used in combination with Jerk Sauce, and works particularly well with pork.

OTHER BACKGROUND INFORMATION: The dry rub was the traditional way of Jerking meat, especially in areas where the 'wet' ingredients of the Jerk Marinade were not as easily available.

INGREDIENTS (ENOUGH FOR SEVERAL DISHES):
1 tbsp grounded pimenta (allspice)
1 tbsp onion powder (or dried onion)
2 tsp salt
2 tsp garlic powder
2 tsp sugar
½ tsp ground cloves
2 tsp dried thyme
¾ tsp ground black pepper
1 tsp (dried) cayenne pepper
¼ tsp ground cinnamon

METHOD:

1. Mix all the dry ingredients in a bowl until well blended.

How to Use Dry Rub:

1. Wash and dry meat/fish in accordance with the full recipe instructions.
2. Place the meat/fish pieces in a dry bowl.
3. Add 1 teaspoon of oil per serving to the meat/fish and rub onto all surfaces.
4. Add approximately 1 teaspoon of Jerk Seasoning per serving to the meat/fish.
5. Rub the seasoning into all surfaces, and ensure that all the surfaces are evenly coated.
6. Store the remaining dry rub in an airtight container for future use.

For best results, marinate meat in dry rub for at least 6 hours, but preferably overnight (24 hours), so that the Jerk Seasoning has time to penetrate the meat.

No. 52 JERK SAUCE

(WET MARINADE)

Most likely to be found in: Jamaica.

THE SECRET: Ground pimenta berries (allspice) and the other spices in the right combination give this dish its unique flavour. Jerk Sauce (along with Jerk Rub) is the key marinade in the making of authentic Jerk Chicken, Jerk Pork and Jerk Fish dishes.

OTHER BACKGROUND INFORMATION: For milder flavour you can use hot pepper sauce (also made from Scotch bonnet peppers) which makes it easier to control.

INGREDIENTS (ENOUGH FOR SEVERAL DISHES):
1 tbsp ground pimenta (allspice)
1 or 2 diced Scotch bonnet or jalapeno peppers, sliced, seeds
    removed for milder flavour
3 tbsp soy sauce
9 escallions/spring onions/green onions, chopped
6 tbsp white vinegar
2 tbsp vegetable oil
2 tbsp chopped fresh thyme
1 bulb (8 cloves) of garlic
½ tsp ground cloves
½ tsp ground nutmeg
1 tsp ginger, diced
1 tsp ground cinnamon
2 tsp ground black pepper
2 tsp lime juice
3 tbsp brown sugar

METHOD:

1. Blend all the ingredients in a food processor until you have a smooth paste.
2. Pass through a sieve, to remove any remaining large pieces of the ingredients.
3. Add one-third (250 ml/9 fl oz) of the Jerk Sauce to chicken pieces and Jerk Rub.
4. Keep one-third (250 ml/9 fl oz) of the Jerk Sauce for basting chicken while cooking.
5. Use the remaining third (250 ml/9 fl oz) of Jerk Sauce to make *Jerk Dipping Sauce* (see overleaf).

No. 53 JERK DIPPING SAUCE

Most likely to be found in: Jamaica.

THE SECRET: This is a simple optional extra for authentic Jerk Chicken.

OTHER BACKGROUND INFORMATION: You can experiment by adding your own ingredients to this recipe. Much depends on how spicy your Jerk Chicken is.

INGREDIENTS (ENOUGH FOR SEVERAL DISHES):
250 ml (1 cup Jerk Sauce)
2 tbsp tomato purée (or tomato ketchup)
3 tbsp white vinegar
1 tbsp brown sugar

METHOD:
1. Add all the ingredients to a saucepan.
2. Cook the ingredients over medium heat for 15–20 minutes.
3. Serve with cooked Jerk Chicken.

No. 54 CARIBBEAN CURRY POWDER

Most likely to be found: All over the Caribbean.

THE SECRET: Caribbean curry powders vary from island to island, so although they all use similar ingredients, they differ widely in quantities and taste.

OTHER BACKGROUND INFORMATION: By making your own seasonings you can eliminate the salt (sodium chloride) which is added in large quantities to the commercially available seasonings.

INGREDIENTS (ENOUGH FOR SEVERAL DISHES):
4 tbsp coriander seeds
1 tbsp fenugreek seeds
1 tbsp black peppercorns
1½ tbsp pimenta (allspice) berries
8 cloves
3 star anise, ground (optional)
1 tbsp turmeric
1½ tbsp garlic powder
1 tbsp ground ginger
1 tbsp dried thyme
1 tbsp brown sugar (optional)
5 cm/2 inch piece cinnamon

METHOD:
1. Combine the seeds, peppercorns, allspice berries, cloves and star anise (optional) in a frying pan.
2. Toast over medium heat until the colour of the spices slightly darkens, and the spices are very fragrant, about 10 minutes.
3. Remove the spices from the pan, and allow to cool to room temperature.
4. Grind the spices with the turmeric in a spice grinder.
5. Add the garlic powder, ginger, thyme, sugar, cinnamon and stir.
6. Store in an airtight container at room temperature.

No. 55 COLOMBO (CURRY) POWDER

Most likely to be found in: Guadeloupe, Martinique,
Saint Martin, Saint Barthélemy.
Alternative Names: French, West Indian Curry Powder,
Poudre De Colombo.

THE SECRET: Black mustard seeds are hotter than white and help to give this curry powder its unique taste. Fenugreek is a spice made up of tiny, rectangular tan pieces with a slight but agreeable bitterness. Both are available in ethnic food stores, markets, gourmet shops, and natural food stores.

OTHER BACKGROUND INFORMATION:

Colombo cooking originated with the Sri Lankan indentured plantation workers in the French West Indies, especially the islands of Martinique and Guadeloupe and is a thick curry-like stew traditionally of lamb or goat.

INGREDIENTS (ENOUGH FOR SEVERAL DISHES):

4 tbsp white long grain rice
4 tbsp cumin seeds (geera)
4 tbsp coriander seeds
3 tbsp black mustard seeds
3 tsp black peppercorns
3 tsp fenugreek seeds
1 tsp whole cloves
4 tbsp turmeric

METHOD:

1. Heat a frying pan over a medium heat and then add the rice.
2. Roast/toast the rice grains for approximately 5 minutes, tossing the pan frequently until the grains are a golden brown.
3. Transfer the toasted grains onto a plate to cool.
4. Add the cumin seeds, coriander seeds, mustard seeds, peppercorns, fenugreek seeds and cloves to the dry frying pan and roast over medium heat for about 3 minutes, tossing the pan frequently to avoid the seeds burning.
5. Transfer the spices to the plate.
6. Grind the rice and roasted spices in a spice grinder/mill or blender into a fine powder. Add the turmeric.
7. Store the Colombo Powder in an airtight container away from light and heat, and use as required. (Shelf life 6–8 months.)

No. 56 CAJUN SEASONING

Most likely to be found in: The French Caribbean and Louisiana.

THE SECRET: Cajun seasoning varies widely from region to region so although they all use similar ingredients, they differ widely in quantities and taste.

OTHER BACKGROUND INFORMATION: By making your own seasonings you can eliminate the salt (sodium chloride) which is added in large quantities to the commercially available seasonings.

INGREDIENTS (ENOUGH FOR SEVERAL DISHES):
3 tbsp white peppercorns
3 tbsp black peppercorns
3 tbsp dried cayenne pepper
3 tbsp paprika (ground)
3 tbsp onion powder
3 tbsp garlic powder

METHOD:
1. In a frying pan toast the peppercorns over medium heat until the colour of the spices slightly darkens, and the spices are very fragrant, about 10 minutes.
2. Remove the spices from the pan, and allow to cool to room temperature.
3. Grind the spices with a spice grinder or coffee grinder.
4. Combine with the powdered ingredients.
5. Store in an airtight container at room temperature.

No. 57 CREOLE SAUCE

Most likely to be found in: The French-speaking
Caribbean and Louisiana.

THE SECRET: The secret of a good Creole sauce is finding the right
blend of tomatoes, celery, bell peppers, onions and garlic, along with
other seasonings and herbs. French Caribbean Creole Sauce recipes
often include coconut milk, which is not an ingredient you will usually
find in Louisianan versions.

INGREDIENTS (ENOUGH FOR SEVERAL DISHES):
½ cup vegetable oil
2 medium onions, chopped
1 medium green pepper, cored, deseeded and finely chopped
2 cloves of garlic
1 tsp finely chopped, deseeded fresh red chilli
3 tsp Creole Seasoning (see overleaf)
1 tsp pepper
3 tomatoes, peeled and chopped
¾ cup/180 ml/6 fl oz tomato paste
½ cup/120 ml/4 fl oz dry white wine
½ cup/120 m/ 4 fl oz coconut milk (option – French
   Caribbean version only)

METHOD:
1. In a medium heavy-based saucepan, heat the oil over low heat. Add
   the onions, green pepper, garlic and chilli; sauté until the peppers are
   soft.
2. Add the Creole Seasoning, pepper and the tomatoes. Cook for about
   10 minutes over low heat, stirring occasionally.
3. Add the tomato paste and wine and simmer, stirring occasionally.
4. Add coconut milk, if you prefer and stir.
5. Serve hot as a pour-over sauce for roasted and grilled meat, fish and
   seafood.

No. 58 CREOLE SEASONING

Most likely to be found in: The French Caribbean and Louisiana.

INGREDIENTS (ENOUGH FOR SEVERAL DISHES):
2 tbsp onion powder
2 tbsp garlic powder
2 tbsp dried oregano
2 tbsp dried basil
3 tsp dried thyme
3 tsp black pepper
3 tsp white pepper
3 tsp cayenne pepper
4 tbsp paprika

METHOD:
1. Combine all the ingredients in a bowl and stir.
2. Store in an airtight container at room temperature.

No. 59 GREEN SEASONING

Most likely to be found in: Trinidad & Tobago and Guyana.
Alternative Name: Paramin Green Seasoning.

THE SECRET: The key ingredient in Green Seasoning is *Chadon Beni* (aka *Shado Beni, culantro* or *Thai Parsley* or *Mexican Parsley*) which can often be found in the larger Oriental supermarkets (Chinese and Thai). If you are unable to find Chadon Beni you can use fresh coriander as a substitute.

OTHER BACKGROUND INFORMATION: Jars/bottles of Green Seasoning are now widely available in ethnic food stores and on the internet. But none of these will beat your own freshly prepared product, so give this recipe a try.

INGREDIENTS (ENOUGH FOR SEVERAL DISHES):
4 large shallots, chopped
1 bunch of chives, minced
1 small bunch fresh thyme, minced
3 tbsp flat-leaf parsley, chopped
2 tbsp Chadon Beni (aka Shado Beni) or coriander (cilantro) leaves, minced
1 medium onion, chopped
4 cloves of garlic, crushed
½ tsp ground black pepper
½ tsp salt
2 tbsp white vinegar

METHOD:
1. Combine all the ingredients in a food processor and purée until smooth (you can add a little water to help, if desired).
2. Either use immediately or store in a sealed glass jar in the refrigerator.
3. Store for up to 1 week.

No. 60 BAJAN SEASONING

Most likely to be found in: Barbados.

THE SECRET: Marjoram (sweet oregano) gives Bajan Seasoning its unique taste. Not to be confused with European oregano this has a sharper taste.

OTHER BACKGROUND INFORMATION: Bajan Seasoning is found in almost every home and is the secret to the success for many mouth-watering Bajan dishes. One of the favourite uses is to place it between the meat and skin of chicken pieces before grilling, baking, or frying.

INGREDIENTS (ENOUGH FOR SEVERAL DISHES):
450 g/1 lb onions, peeled and coarsely chopped
5 escallion/green onion stalks, chopped
6 cloves of garlic, peeled
2 Scotch bonnet/habanero peppers, seeds and stems removed
2 sprigs of fresh thyme
50 g/2 oz fresh parsley
50 g/2 oz fresh sweet marjoram
1 cup/240 ml/8 fl oz vinegar
2 tbsp Worcestershire sauces
1 tsp ground cloves
¼ tsp black pepper
2 fresh limes, squeezed

METHOD:
1. Add the onions, escallions, garlic and hot peppers to a food processor and blend into a rough paste.
2. Remove the leaves from the stems of the thyme, parsley, and sweet marjoram.
3. Add the herbs to the food processor together with the vinegar and blend for 1–2 minutes until the ingredients are liquefied.
4. Combine with all the remaining ingredients in a bowl and stir.
5. Cover the mixture and place in the refrigerator for 1 week before first use.
6. Use Bajan Seasoning as required for Barbadian recipes.
7. Refrigerate after use, and store for up to 6 months.

No. 61 FISH CHOWDER

(NATIONAL DISH: BERMUDA)

Most likely to be found in: Bermuda, the Bahamas.

THE SECRET: When making your own fish stock it is important to wash the fish bones thoroughly and simmer the stock on the lowest heat in order to prevent the stock going cloudy. Also do not add the fish fillets too early as the natural flavour of the fish can evaporate into broth.

OTHER BACKGROUND INFORMATION: Bermudian Fish Chowder is served with local favourites *Outerbridge's Sherry Rum Pepper Sauce* and *Gosling's Black Seal Rum.*

INGREDIENTS (SERVES 6):
For Fish Stock:
1 Sachet d'épices (bag of herbs)
2 bay leaves
2 sprigs of fresh thyme
10 peppercorns
6 whole cloves
1 piece of cheese cloth (10 cm/4 inches square)

2.25 kg/5 lb fish bones (excluding bones of oily fish)
4 tbsp unsalted butter
3 medium onions, chopped
3 sticks of celery, chopped
2 carrots, chopped
2 cloves of garlic, minced
5 cups/1.2 litres/2 pints cold water
2 green peppers, chopped

For Fish Chowder:
1 medium onion, chopped
2 green peppers, chopped
2 cloves of garlic, minced
1 x 400 g can/tin chopped tomatoes (including juice)
1 x 400 g can/tin beef consommé
¼ cup/60 ml/2 fl oz tomato ketchup

1 tbsp Worcestershire Sauce
4 large potatoes, (about 900 g/2 lb), peeled and diced
6 sticks of celery, diced
6 carrots, diced
680 g/1½ lb fish fillets (bluefish, rockfish, snapper or whitefish)

Optional Ingredients:
1 cup shrimps/prawns
1 cup clams

To Serve:
2–4 tbsp pepper sauce (to taste)
¼ cup/60 ml/2 fl oz dark rum
½–1 tsp black ground pepper (to taste)
½ tsp salt (to taste)
2 lemons, cut into wedges (to taste)
chopped parsley (for garnish)

METHOD:
Fish Stock:
1. Make a bag of herbs (sachet d'épices) by tying the bay leaves, thyme, peppercorns and cloves into a piece of cheesecloth.
2. Wash the fish bones removing any blood which could make the stock cloudy.
3. Melt the butter in a Dutch Pot/heavy-bottomed pan.
4. Add the chopped onions, celery, carrots and garlic, and sauté for 5 minutes.
5. Add the fish bones, water and bag of herbs and bring to the boil.
6. Reduce the heat to low and lightly simmer for 30 minutes.
7. While the stock is simmering use a large spoon to skim off any oil or impurities that rise to the top of the pan.
8. Remove the stock from the heat and strain.
9. Discard the fish bones and vegetables, and set the stock to one side.

Prepare Fish Chowder:
1. Add the chopped onion, green peppers and minced garlic to the pot and sauté for 5 minutes.
2. Add the stock, tomatoes, consommé, ketchup, Worcestershire Sauce, potatoes, celery, and carrots and bring to the boil.
3. Simmer, partially covered, for 1–1½ hours.

4. Ten minutes prior to serving add the fish fillets, shrimps/prawns and/or clams if used.
5. Before serving, garnish the fish chowder with chopped fresh parsley.

No. 62 SWEET POTATOES ROASTED IN HERBS

Most likely to be found: All over the Caribbean.

THE SECRET: A very simple dish which is full of flavour.

OTHER BACKGROUND INFORMATION: Sweet potato is a very versatile dish which can be roasted, boiled or mashed. It's widely used in Caribbean Sunday dinners.

INGREDIENTS (SERVES 6):
1.5 kg/3 lb sweet potatoes
1 large onion
2 tbsp chopped fresh herbs (rosemary, chives, thyme, parsley)
3 tbsp olive oil
2 tbsp butter melted
1 clove of garlic, finely chopped
¼ tsp salt and ground black pepper

METHOD:
1. Preheat the oven to 450°F/230°C /Gas mark 8.
2. Lightly oil a baking dish and set aside.
3. Peel, wash and cut the potatoes into 2.5–3.75 cm/1–1½ inch cubes. Peel and chop the onion
4. Put the herbs, sweet potatoes and onion in the dish.
5. Combine the oil, melted butter, garlic, salt and pepper, in a small bowl and drizzle over the potatoes. Mix together.
6. Bake in the oven for 30 minutes, stir, bake for 10 minutes more then toss well.
7. Continue to bake for a further 10–15 minutes until the sweet potatoes are tender and brown.

No. 63 GRIOTS (PORK) WITH RICE & BEANS

(NATIONAL DISH: HAITI)

Most likely to be found in: Haiti and all over the Caribbean.
Alternative Names: Haitian Pork Shoulder
with Rice & Beans; Griots, Riz et Pois.

THE SECRET: The double-cooking of the pork (boiled and then fried) is the secret to this wonderful dish.

OTHER BACKGROUND INFORMATION: This dish can be served with rice and beans or Haitian Black Mushroom Rice (riz djondjon) and Fried Plantain (bananas pesees). Many Haitians like to eat griots (pork) with their very hot *Ti-Malice* sauce.

INGREDIENTS (SERVES 6):
For Pork:
1.3 kg/3 lb shoulder of pork, cut into 2.5–5 cm/1–2 inch cubes
3 tbsp vinegar/lime juice
1 large onion, finely chopped
½ cup shallots, chopped
1 cup/240 ml/8 fl oz bitter orange juice
1 hot green pepper, chopped
1 tsp salt
1 tsp black pepper
1 tsp chopped thyme
½ cup vegetable oil

For Rice & Beans:
2 tbsp vegetable oil
1 onion, finely chopped
2 shallots, chopped
1 green pepper, chopped
1 tbsp butter
400g tin/can red kidney beans
3 cups water (approx.)
2 cups/400 g/14 oz long grain rice
salt (to taste)

METHOD:
For the Pork:
1. Prepare the pork using the vinegar/lime juice (optional). (See: *Meat and Fish Preparation – Caribbean Style*, page 9.)
2. Put all the ingredients, except the oil in a large pot and marinate overnight in the refrigerator.
3. Place the pot with the marinated pork on the stove; and add water to cover all the ingredients.
4. Simmer for 90 minutes.
5. Once cooked, drain the mixture.
6. Add the oil to a frying pan and fry the pork until brown and caramelized on the outside.

Prepare Rice and Beans:
1. Heat the vegetable oil in a pan, and then add the chopped onion, shallots and green pepper.
2. When the onion is tender, add the butter and kidney beans (together with the water in the tin) and season to taste.
3. Add the water and bring to the boil.
4. Add the rice and bring back to the boil.
5. Reduce the heat to its lowest setting, cover the pot with tin foil and the lid and then cook for 20–25 minutes until the rice is soft and fluffy. Add salt to taste.
6. Serve with the griots (pork).

No. 64 AJIACO CUBANO

(CUBAN STEW)

Most likely to be found in: Cuba and South America.
Alternative Name: Cuban Root Vegetable Stew.

THE SECRET: There are many processes to this dish, so you will need to be patient and organized to get it right. This is a hearty meat stew which is a complete one-pot dish. The secret of any good Cuban dish is the *'sofrito'* (base cooking sauce) which is a combination of crushed garlic, diced onions and sweet peppers and tomatoes which are slowly sautéed or braised in olive oil until the main ingredients form a smooth thick sauce.

OTHER BACKGROUND INFORMATION: Dried beef jerky is widely available in most large food superstores or online.

INGREDIENTS (SERVES 8–10):
Meats:
225 g/½ lb beef jerky
5 cups/1.2 litres/2 pints water
680 g/1½ lb chicken pieces, chopped
450 g/1 lb flank steak, cubed
450 g/1 lb pork spareribs, separated

Vegetables (Viandas):
2 ears of corn, cut in four pieces
450 g/1 lb yellow taro root, peeled, cut in chunks
450 g/1 lb cassava, cut in chunks
450 g/1 lb sweet potato, peeled and cut in chunks
225 g/½ lb white taro root, peeled and cut in chunks
225 g/½ lb grey taro root, peeled and cut in chunks
2 ripe plantain, peeled and cut in chunks
450 g/1 lb pumpkin/butternut squash, peeled and cut in chunks
2 green plantain (green fig/green banana), chopped and soaked in lime juice.
2 fresh limes or 2 tbsp lime juice (for soaking the green plantains)

salt (to taste)
1 tsp ground black pepper

Sofrito (Base Cooking Sauce/Seasoning):
2 tbsp olive oil
1 onion, fine dice
5 escallions, fine dice
1 large green pepper, fine dice
4 cloves of garlic, minced
2 tsp oregano
½ tsp ground cumin (geera)
2 bay leaves (whole)
1 tsp salt (to taste)
1 tsp ground black pepper
1 tube of tomato purée (130–150 g)

METHOD:
NB: Cut the beef jerky in large pieces and soak overnight in enough water to cover prior to use.

Prepare the Soup:
1. Drain the water off the beef jerky and place in a very large and deep stockpot.
2. Add the 5 cups of water and the cut up chicken.
3. Boil the chicken and beef jerky on medium heat for 1 hour.
4. Add the flank steak and pork spareribs.
5. Boil for one more hour.
6. Remove the fat and froth that will rise to the top of the stockpot.
7. While the meats are cooking, peel and cut the vegetables, and make the Sofrito (sauce/seasoning).

Prepare Sofrito (Sauce/Seasoning):
1. In a frying pan heat the oil and then add onion and escallions and green pepper, and cook for 10 minutes.
2. Add the garlic, herbs and tomato purée to the pan and allow to simmer on low heat for a further 15–20 minutes.
3. Remove and discard the bay leaves.

Prepare the Vegetables:

1. When the meats are tender, add the vegetables, except for the ripe plantains and pumpkin.
2. Cook for about one hour more.
3. Add the seasoning and cook another for 20–30 minutes.
4. Add the ripe plantains and pumpkin and cook for 30 more minutes or until the pumpkin and plantains are tender.
5. Taste for seasoning and adjust if necessary.
6. If the broth is too thin, thicken by removing some of the vegetables from the pot, mashing them and then adding them back into the pot.

Serve:

This dish can be served as a stew with rice and salad or as a soup.

No. 65 BOILED GROUND PROVISIONS

Most likely to be found: All over the Caribbean.
Alternative Name: Boiled Hard Food.

THE SECRET: Cooking a selection of Ground Provisions together takes practice. Some yams, for example, take longer to cook than Ground Provisions such as dasheen and cassava, so you may wish to add them to the cooking pot first.

OTHER BACKGROUND INFORMATION: Cutting vegetables to an equal size will ensure that they cook evenly and do not fall apart. There are many different varieties of yams.

INGREDIENTS (SERVES 6):
2 pints/1.1 litres approx. water (enough to cover vegetables)
2 tsp salt (to taste)
1 medium sized yam, peeled and cut into equal size pieces
   (sufficient for 6 servings)
3 green bananas/green figs, peeled and cut in half
1 medium-sized dasheen, peeled and cut into equal size pieces
2 medium-sized cassava, peeled and cut into equal size pieces
2 medium-sized sweet potatoes, peeled and cut into equal size
   pieces

METHOD:
1. Heat the water in a large saucepan, add salt and bring to the boil.
2. Add the yam and green bananas.
3. After 5 minutes add all the other root vegetables to the pan.
4. Bring back to the boil then reduce the heat to simmer.
5. Cook for about 25–45 minutes (testing regularly) until the Ground Provisions will slide off a fork easily.
6. If a particular Ground Provision is cooked before the others, remove from the pan and set aside.
7. Serve with any Caribbean meat or fish dish as an alternative to rice.

No. 66 RASTA PASTA

Most likely to be found in: Jamaica, and all over the Caribbean.
Alternative Name: Pasta in a Spicy Tomato Sauce.

THE SECRET: The secret to any good pasta dish is not overcooking the pasta. Some recipes suggest that you bake the pasta for 20 minutes plus rather than grill, but this will only ruin the pasta.

OTHER BACKGROUND INFORMATION: Rasta Pasta is a simple but very colourful dish. It is said to have obtained its name from the three different colours of sweet peppers (red, green and yellow) used in the dish, which are also the colours of the Rastafarian movement.

INGREDIENTS (SERVES 6):
600 g/1 lb 5 oz pasta shapes (macaroni, penne, fusilli or
    farfalle)
3 tbsp butter, divided into 3 portions
4 chicken breasts, boned, skinned, trimmed and cut into
    0.5 cm/¼ inch slices
2 tbsp Cajun seasoning
4 cloves of garlic, crushed
1 large red onion, cut into wedges
1 green pepper, deseeded and sliced into strips
1 red pepper, deseeded and sliced into strips
1 yellow pepper, deseeded and sliced into strips
1 tsp crushed red pepper flakes or hot pepper sauce
¼ tsp Caribbean curry powder
salt and pepper (to taste)
2 x 12 oz jars tomato & basil pesto sauce (or 1 x tube of
    tomato purée seasoned with 2 tsp of fresh basil)
3 tsp cheese (Parmesan, Cheddar or any other medium tasting
    cheese of your choosing), grated

METHOD:

1. Bring a large pot of lightly salted water to a boil.
2. Add the pasta and cook until tender but still firm, about 8 minutes. Drain.
3. Meanwhile, melt 1 tablespoon of the butter in another pan over medium-high heat.
4. Add the chicken pieces; cook and stir until browned.
5. Season with the Cajun seasoning, and remove the chicken from the pan and set aside.
6. Melt the second portion of the butter in the pan over medium-high heat.
7. Add the garlic and onion; cook and stir until fragrant and beginning to brown.
8. Add the green, red and yellow pepper strips, and season with red pepper flakes (or pepper sauce), curry powder, salt and pepper.
9. Cook and stir until the peppers are hot.
10. Return the chicken to the pan and pour in the pesto sauce.
11. Melt the remaining piece of butter in an oven-proof dish, and then use a brush to coat all the inside surfaces of the dish.
12. Add the pasta to the dish.
13. Sprinkle Parmesan cheese over the pasta and then grill until the cheese is golden brown.
14. Remove the dish from the grill and serve.

No. 67 CORNMEAL PORRIDGE

Most likely to be found in: Jamaica.

THE SECRET: Cornmeal porridge is a Caribbean favourite, but its thickness varies greatly. Sweetened condensed milk is widely used in Caribbean porridges, but brown sugar is a more than adequate substitute.

ADDITIONAL SECRET: Coarse cornmeal (polenta) is made from maize which has been milled and cleaned to ensure it is free from any impurities. It is widely used in Caribbean cooking to make porridge, cornbread, festivals.

OTHER BACKGROUND INFORMATION: Cornmeal (polenta) is a coarse flour ground from dried maize (corn) to fine, medium or coarse consistencies. Remember cornmeal (polenta) is not the same thing as cornstarch or cornflour!

You can add butter to this porridge to enhance the flavour. Cinnamon can be used as a 'false sweetener' to trick the taste buds into believing that something is sweeter than it really is. Therefore, by increasing the amount of cinnamon in this dish and reducing the amount of sugar you can increase the flavour and reduce the calories in this porridge. This will give you a nice light flavour instead of that heavy sugar taste.

INGREDIENTS (SERVES 6):
½ tsp salt
5 cups/1.2 litres/2 pints water
1 cup yellow cornmeal/polenta (fine or coarse)
1 cup/240 ml/8 fl oz milk
1 tsp vanilla essence
½ tsp ground cinnamon
¼ ground nutmeg
2 tbsp condensed milk or 2 tbsp brown sugar (to sweeten, optional)

METHOD:

1. Place the salt and water into a pan and bring to the boil.
2. Place the cornmeal in a separate bowl.
3. Add the milk to the cornmeal and slowly stir into a smooth paste.
4. Stir the cornmeal paste into the boiling salted water.
5. Cover and cook on a low heat for 10–15 minutes.
6. Stir in the vanilla, cinnamon and nutmeg. Cover and simmer for 15 more minutes.
7. Sweeten with the condensed milk or sugar.
8. Serve hot with hard dough bread.

No. 68 CURRIED PUMPKIN & CALLALOO

Most likely to be found: All over the Caribbean.

THE SECRET: This is a very simple dish which is difficult to spoil.

OTHER BACKGROUND INFORMATION: If you are not a fan of pumpkin, you can use butternut squash instead.

INGREDIENTS (SERVES 6):
225 g/½ lb callaloo
1 tbsp oil (for frying)
1 medium onion, diced
2 tbsp Caribbean curry powder
4 cloves of garlic, minced
1 tbsp chopped fresh/dried thyme
3 escallion stalks, diced
1½ cups/360 ml/12 fl oz boiling water/vegetable stock/bouillon
0.5 kg/1¼ lb pumpkin or butternut squash, peeled and cut into cubes
1 tsp lemon juice
salt and pepper (to taste)
hot sauce (for serving, optional)

METHOD:

1. Wash the callaloo thoroughly to remove any grit and leave to soak while preparing the other ingredients.
2. In a Dutch pot/heavy-bottomed pan heat the oil.
3. Add the diced onion to the pot and sauté for a couple of minutes.
4. Add the curry powder, garlic, thyme and escallion and cook for a further minute, stirring constantly.
5. Add the boiled water or vegetable stock to the pot and stir continuously until you get a thick curry sauce.
6. Add the chopped pumpkin (or butternut squash) and stir to coat with the curry.
7. Add additional hot water, if necessary, and simmer for 20 minutes.
8. Mash a few pieces of the pumpkin against the side of the pot to thicken the sauce.
9. Once the pumpkin is almost cooked, drain the callaloo, dice it and add to the pot.
10. Cook for a further 5–10 minutes until the water reduces down, the vegetables are tender, and the curry sauce is thick.
11. Add the lemon juice and stir.
12. Add salt and pepper (to taste).
13. Serve with rotis, rice and/or curried meat or fish.

No. 69 CURRY CHICKEN

Most likely to be found: All over the Caribbean.
Alternative Names: Curried Chicken, Caribbean Chicken Curry.

THE SECRET: The meat in Caribbean curries is marinated in the curry spices for several hours (or overnight) and then slow cooked for a deep, rice curry flavour.

OTHER BACKGROUND INFORMATION: The Jamaican version of this recipe uses less curry powder than the Trinidadian version. The Trinidadian version also includes Green Seasoning (see: *Essential Caribbean Ingredients* and Recipe No. 59).

INGREDIENTS (SERVES 6):
1.3 kg/3 lb chicken pieces or 1 whole chicken, cut into
    8 pieces
2 limes, squeezed (optional)
1 medium onion, chopped
1 tsp salt
1 tsp hot pepper sauce or 1 Scotch bonnet pepper, whole or
    fine dice (to taste)
4 cloves of garlic, crushed

Jamaican Version:
2 tbsp Jamaican curry powder

Trinidadian Version:
4 tbsp Trinidadian curry powder
2 tbsp Green Seasoning
½ cup tomatoes, chopped

50 ml/2 fl oz cooking oil
100 ml/4 fl oz water
1 tsp black pepper (optional)
1 sprig of thyme, finely diced (optional)
1 tsp grated ginger (optional)
1 potato, cut in eight pieces (optional)

METHOD:

1. Prepare the chicken using lime juice (optional). (See: *Meat and Fish Preparation – Caribbean Style*, page 9.)
2. Remove the excess liquid.
3. With a sharp knife trim off any excess fat, skin or sinew.
4. Place the chicken portions in a bowl.
5. Combine the chicken with the onion, salt, hot pepper sauce or Scotch bonnet pepper, garlic, and either 1 tablespoon of Jamaican curry powder or 2 tablespoons of Trinidadian curry powder and Green Seasoning.
6. Leave to marinade in the refrigerator for several hours or preferably overnight.
7. Remove the chicken from the refrigerator.
8. Add the cooking oil to a Dutch Pot and turn the heat to high.
9. Add 1 tablespoon of Jamaican curry powder or 2 tablespoons of Trinidadian curry powder to the oil and cook until the curry powder changes colour to a darker brown.
10. Add the chicken to the hot oil and brown the chicken.
11. Reduce the heat to medium heat and add the water, black pepper (optional), thyme, grated ginger and chopped tomatoes (Trinidadian version).
12. Cook for 20–30 minutes, add the potato then cover the pot and simmer for a further 15 minutes.
13. Taste and correct seasoning as necessary.
14. Serve with rice and/or roti.

No. 70 CUCUMBER CHUTNEY

Most likely to be found in: Trinidad & Tobago.

THE SECRET: This is a very simple chutney with Chadon Beni as its special, authentic ingredient. If you are unable to obtain the Chadon Beni herb you can always use fresh coriander (cilantro) as a substitute.

OTHER BACKGROUND INFORMATION: Cucumber Chutney is just one of the many accompaniments that can be served with Trinidadian Doubles. Others include Caribbean hot pepper sauce and mango chutney.

INGREDIENTS (SERVES 6):
1 large cucumber
¼ tsp brown sugar
2 tsp lime or lemon juice
3 cloves of garlic
1 tbsp Chadon Beni
1 tbsp chives
1 Scotch bonnet pepper, diced or 1 tsp Caribbean hot pepper sauce (to taste)
½ tsp salt (to taste)
½ black pepper (to taste)

METHOD:

1. Cut the cucumber from top to tail into 4 equal quarters and then cut each quarter into half.

2. Remove the cucumber seeds (but leave on the skin for colour) from all 8 pieces of cucumber and then either finely dice or grate the cucumber into relatively small pieces.

3. Add the brown sugar and lime/lemon juice to the cucumber to stop the flesh turning brown.

4. Finely dice the garlic, Chadon Beni and chives and add to the mix.

5. Add the finely diced Scotch bonnet pepper or hot pepper sauce, stir and season to taste.

6. Serve as an accompaniment with Trinidadian Doubles.

No. 71 PHULORIE [PULL-OW-REE]

Most likely to be found in: Trinidad & Tobago, and Guyana.
Alternative Names: Pholourie, Savoury Split Pea Fritter Balls.

THE SECRET: The key ingredient is split pea/dhal powder/flour, which is quite difficult to find in the UK. However, you can always make your own or use Chana Dhal (chickpea) flour as an alternative.

In the Guyanese recipe the ratio of split pea powder to plain/all-purpose flour is 2:1 whereas in the Trinidadian recipe it is 2:½.

Most recipes advise against using hot pepper sauce in the Phulorie batter, so use fresh chillies or other hot peppers (to taste) here.

OTHER BACKGROUND INFORMATION: You may be able to find one of the following Trinidadian split pea powder brands at your local ethnic food store or market: *Lions Brand, Chatak* or *Sheik.*

INGREDIENTS (SERVES 6):
Trinidadian Version:
2 cups split pea powder/flour or 2 cups ground split peas
½ cup/75 g/2½ oz plain/all-purpose flour
2 cloves garlic, minced/puréed
1 tsp salt
black pepper
1 tsp Caribbean curry powder
1 tsp cumin (geera)
2 tsp baking powder
1 small hot pepper, finely diced, (to taste)

Guyanese Version:
2 cups dhal (split peas) flour
1 cup/150 g/5 oz plain flour
3 cloves garlic
1 onion, finely diced
1 tsp salt
3 tsp baking powder
2 tsp curry powder
½ red Scotch bonnet pepper, diced and seeds removed

METHOD:

NB. If you cannot find split pea powder/flour you will need to soak your split peas overnight, dry, and then grind into a fine powder using an electric grinder or hand-grinder on its finest setting.

1. Mix the split pea powder, flour and other dry ingredients, plus Scotch bonnet/hot pepper into a bowl.
2. Add enough water to make a thick batter, and allow to stand for at least 1 hour.
3. Heat some oil for frying in a Dutch Pot, wok or other round-bottomed pan.
4. Drop a teaspoonful of batter at a time into the hot oil, and let it cook until puffed and making golden brown balls. (**TIP:** You can fry several phulorie balls at the same time, but not too many as it will make it more difficult to maintain the right temperature of the oil.)
5. Serve with Tamarind Sauce, Caribbean Mango Chutney and/or Caribbean hot pepper sauce.
6. The Guyanese version of this recipe may also be served with '*Mango Sour*' which is made by:
   a) Peeling 1 or 2 green mangos, and cutting them into large slices.
   b) In a covered pan, steaming the mango slices on medium/low heat with 2 or 3 cloves of garlic, 1 teaspoon of hot pepper sauce and 1 teaspoon of salt, plus enough water to cover the mango slices.
   c) Adding extra water (as necessary) to prevent the ingredients burning/drying.
   d) When the mango is soft, removing it from the heat, cooling, and then blending in a food processor.

No. 72 CURRIED CHICKPEAS & POTATOES

Most likely to be found in: Trinidad & Tobago and Guyana.
Alternative Name: Curry Channa and Aloo.

THE SECRET: This is a very simple dish, but the flavour can be improved if the potatoes are marinated in the curry spices for a few hours before cooking. The potatoes and chickpeas can easily be substituted with pumpkin and callaloo.

OTHER BACKGROUND INFORMATION: Precooked canned/tinned chickpeas are now widely available in most food stores, which eliminates the need to soak and boil dried chickpeas.

INGREDIENTS (SERVES 6):
1 tbsp oil (for frying)
1 medium onion, diced
2 tbsp Caribbean curry powder
4 cloves of garlic, minced
1 tbsp chopped fresh/dried thyme
3 escallion stalks, diced
1½ cups/360 ml/12 fl oz boiling water/vegetable
    stock/bouillon
2 potatoes, peeled and cut into cubes
1 x 400 g tin chickpeas
salt and pepper (to taste)
hot sauce for serving (optional)

METHOD:

1. In a Dutch Pot/heavy-bottomed pan, heat the oil.
2. Add the diced onion to the pot and sauté for a couple of minutes.
3. Add the curry powder, garlic, thyme and escallion and cook for a further minute, stirring constantly.
4. Add 2–3 tablespoons of the water/vegetable stock to the pot and stir continuously until you get a thick curry sauce.
5. Add the chopped potatoes and stir them to coat with the curry.
6. Add additional boiling water, if necessary, to maintain a simmer.
7. Mash a few potatoes against the side of the pot to thicken the sauce.
8. Add the drained chickpeas and mix.
9. Cook until the water reduces down, the vegetables are tender, and the curry sauce is thick.
10. Add salt and pepper (to taste).
11. Serve with rotis, Doubles and/or other curried meats.

No. 73 CREOLE RICE

Most likely to be found: All over the Caribbean and Louisiana.

THE SECRET: The secret of a great Creole (or Cajun) dish is what is known as the 'Creole (or Cajun) holy trinity' (a *mirepoix* of vegetables) being the blend of onions, bell peppers and celery which form the basis of the dish.

OTHER BACKGROUND INFORMATION: In many Louisianan Creole and Cajun recipes the 'holy trinity' of vegetable ingredients are added in equal quantities. However, this is not necessarily the case in Eastern Caribbean Creole or Cajun cooking, so you are free to experiment with whatever quantities you prefer.

INGREDIENTS (SERVES 6):
2 tsp vegetable oil
1 large onion, finely diced
100 g/¼ lb bacon (optional), finely chopped
2 cloves of garlic, chopped
1 small red sweet pepper, finely diced
1 small green pepper, finely diced
2 sticks of celery, finely diced
1 tbsp chopped fresh thyme
1 tsp Creole Seasoning (see: Recipe No. 58)
1 tsp hot pepper sauce (to taste)
1 x 400 g tin/can chopped tomatoes or 4 medium fresh
    tomatoes, diced
2 cups/400 g/14 oz long grain rice
2½ cups/600 ml/1 pint stock (vegetable, beef or chicken)
1 x 400 ml tin/can coconut milk (optional Caribbean Creole
    – to be *substituted* for 400ml of the water or stock)

METHOD:

1. Heat the oil in a heavy-bottomed pan on medium heat.
2. Add the onion and bacon (optional), cook until the onion is soft.
3. Add the garlic, diced sweet peppers, diced celery and thyme.
4. Add the Creole Seasoning and hot pepper sauce and stir.
5. Add the tomatoes, stir and cook for 5 minutes.
6. Add the rice, and stir into the other ingredients.
7. Add the stock and coconut milk⋆ (⋆as a partial substitute for the stock).
8. Cover with tin foil and the lid, then steam for 15–20 minutes until all the liquid has been absorbed and the rice is cooked.
9. Add salt, to taste.
10. Serve with any Caribbean meat or fish dish as an alternative to rice and peas, and/or Ground Provisions.

No. 74 CALYPSO RICE

Alternative Name: Trini Calypso Rice
Most likely to be found in: Trinidad & Tobago.

INGREDIENTS (SERVES 6):
2 tsp vegetable oil
1 small onion, finely diced
2 cloves of garlic, chopped
1 tsp hot pepper sauce (to taste)
1 small red sweet pepper, finely diced
1 small green pepper, finely diced
1 carrot, finely diced
1 tbsp chopped fresh thyme
2 cups/400 g/14 oz long grain rice
2 cups/480 ml/16 fl oz water
2 cups/480 ml/16 fl oz stock (vegetable or chicken)
1 tsp salt (to taste)

METHOD:
1. Heat the oil in a heavy-bottomed pan on medium heat.
2. Add the onion to the pan and heat until soft.
3. Add the garlic, hot pepper sauce, diced sweet peppers, diced carrot and thyme.
4. Add the rice to the other ingredients in the pot and then stir for 1 minute.
5. Add the water and stock.
6. Cover and steam for 15–20 minutes until all the liquid has been absorbed and the rice is cooked.
7. Serve with any Caribbean meat or fish dish as an alternative to rice and peas, and/or Ground Provisions.

No. 75 CALLALOO FRITTERS

Most likely to be found in: Jamaica.

THE SECRET: Do not use too much oil in the frying process, as this will make the fritters too greasy. Also, the oil must be hot enough, so that the fritters do not absorb too much of it. Milk creates a smoother batter than water. You also tend to get better results if you use a food processor to blend the batter ingredients.

OTHER BACKGROUND INFORMATION: Caribbean Fritters can be served hot or cold for breakfast or lunch, or as a starter for an evening meal.

INGREDIENTS (SERVES 6):
3 onions
1 chilli pepper, deseeded
1 small sweet pepper, deseeded
1 bunch callaloo
1 tsp black pepper
2 sprigs of thyme, chopped
750 g/1½ lb self-raising flour or half plain, half self-raising
1 tsp sugar
25 g/1 oz butter
½ tsp salt
285 ml/½ pint milk
oil for shallow frying

METHOD:
1. Wash and chop the onions, peppers and callaloo.
2. Put in a blender along with the black pepper and thyme and blend.
3. Put the flour, sugar, butter, salt and milk in a bowl and mix together with the blended vegetables.
4. Heat 1 tsp of the oil in a shallow frying pan and fry small amounts of the batter to make 3 or 4 fritters at a time. Fry until golden brown on each side.
5. Remove the cooked fritters from the pan and drain on kitchen roll.
6. Repeat Steps 4 and 5 until all the batter mixture is finished.

No. 76 SALT FISH FRITTERS

Most likely to be found in: Jamaica, Trinidad and all over the Caribbean.

THE SECRET: As with Callaloo Fritters, do not use too much oil in the frying process, as this will make the fritters too greasy. Also, make sure the oil is hot enough so that the fritters do not absorb too much oil. Milk creates a smoother batter than water. You also tend to get better results if you use a food processor to blend the batter ingredients.

OTHER BACKGROUND INFORMATION: Fritters may also be shallow or deep fried, but do ensure that the oil is hot and that individual fritters have enough space in the frying pan or deep fat fryer to ensure quick and even cooking.

If using dried salt fish, it must be presoaked in water for several hours (or overnight) prior to cooking. For more information, see: *Salted Fish* in *Essential Caribbean Cooking Ingredients*, page 16.

INGREDIENTS (SERVES 6):
225 g/½ lb salt fish/salted cod (dried or tinned)
1 medium sized onion, finely diced
2 green onions, chopped
½ sweet red/green pepper, finely diced
1 tsp black pepper
½ cup/120 ml/4 fl oz milk or water
1 tsp baking powder
150 g/5 oz/1 cup plain/all-purpose flour (or half plain and
    half self-raising)
oil (for frying)
1 Scotch bonnet pepper, seeds removed and diced
salt (to taste)

METHOD:

1. If using dried salt fish: Soak the salt fish overnight in water or for at least 6-8 hours (changing the water at least 3-4 times) to remove excess salt.
2. If used tinned salt fish: Go to Step 4.
3. Taste a small piece of the salt fish prior to use to check that it is not too salty. Change water and soak for a further 2 hours, if necessary.
4. Using a sharp knife, dice the salt fish into equal size pieces, and add to a clean mixing bowl.
5. Add the finely diced onions, sweet pepper and black pepper to the salt fish and stir.
6. Pour in the milk (or water) and stir.
7. Allow this mixture to stand for 30 minutes before adding the baking powder and flour.
8. Mix until everything is blended into a smooth, thick batter.
9. Heat 1 tsp of the oil in a shallow frying pan and fry small amounts of the batter to make 3 or 4 fritters at a time. Fry until golden brown on each side.
10. Remove the cooked fritters from the pan and drain on kitchen roll.
11. Repeat Steps 4 and 5 until all the batter mixture is finished.

No. 77 CARIBBEAN STEAMED STIR FRIED CABBAGE & CARROTS

Most likely to be found: All over the Caribbean.

THE SECRET: The secret is to ensure that the cabbage and carrots are not overcooked (soggy).

OTHER BACKGROUND INFORMATION: This is a very simple dish which can be served with any Caribbean main course.

INGREDIENTS (SERVES 6):
1 medium hard cabbage
225 g/½ lb carrots
1 onion
1 sweet pepper (any colour)
50 ml/2 fl oz oil (for frying)
3 rashers of bacon, diced (optional)
1 whole Scotch bonnet pepper or 1½ tsp hot pepper sauce
2 tomatoes
225 g/½ lb mushrooms (optional)
1 sprig of fresh thyme
1 tsp mixed herbs
pinch salt/black pepper (to taste)
1–2 tbsp water

METHOD:

1. Wash and shred the cabbage and carrots.
2. Clean and chop the onion and sweet pepper. The Scotch bonnet pepper should not be chopped but cooked whole.
3. Heat a wok or pot on a high heat and then add the oil.
4. Add the onion, and bacon if using, and stir for 2–3 minutes.
5. Add the cabbage, carrots and peppers and/or hot pepper sauce, and stir for a further 2–3 minutes.
6. Add the tomatoes, mushrooms (if using), thyme, mixed herbs, salt and black pepper and stir.
7. Add the water, reduce the heat and cover.
8. Cook for 12–15 minutes until the cabbage and carrots are cooked.
9. Serve hot.

No. 78 CREOLE CHICKEN

Most likely to be found in: The French-speaking
eastern Caribbean and Louisiana.

THE SECRET: The 'trinity of vegetables' (onions, celery and peppers)
is the secret of any good Creole dish. Also a good Creole Seasoning is
very important. You can attempt to make your own or buy it ready made
in most food stores and markets.

OTHER BACKGROUND INFORMATION: Creole food is greatly
influenced by French settlers but also has significant traces of African,
English, German, Native American, Portuguese and Spanish cooking.

INGREDIENTS (SERVES 4–6):
either 8 pieces of chicken (legs and thighs) or 1 whole
    chicken, cut into portions
4–6 tsp Creole Seasoning (to taste), see: Recipe No. 58
2 small onions, diced
1 stick of celery, diced
1 green pepper, diced
1 Scotch bonnet pepper, deseeded and chopped or 2 tsp hot
    pepper sauce (to taste) or ½ fresh jalapeno pepper
6–10 small mushrooms, chopped (optional)
5 cloves of garlic, minced
1 tbsp vegetable oil (for frying)
1 x 400 g can/tin chopped tomatoes, with liquid
white/black pepper (to taste)

METHOD:
1. Season/Marinade the chicken pieces with the Creole Seasoning for 4–6 hours (or preferably overnight).
2. In a Dutch Pot or deep frying pan, sauté the diced onions, celery, green pepper, hot pepper/hot pepper sauce, mushrooms and garlic in the oil on high heat for 3–5 minutes.
3. Add the chicken pieces and brown for a further 2–3 minutes.
4. Add the tomatoes and stir.
5. Reduce the heat, cover and slow cook for 1 hour until the chicken is well done. (**NB**: If you wish to cook this dish the Louisianan way you can use a ready-made slow cooker which will add several hours more to the cooking time.)
6. Serve with rice, salad and/or Ground Provisions.

No. 79: CREOLE JAMBALAYA

Most likely to be found in: New Orleans, Louisiana.
Alternative Name: Red Jambalaya.

THE SECRET: As with other Creole cookery, the secret of a good Jambalaya is the 'Holy Trinity' of vegetables (onions, celery and peppers). You can alter the proportions to suit your own individual taste.

OTHER BACKGROUND INFORMATION: Creole is a blend of French, Spanish, African, Portuguese, Italian and Native American cooking.

INGREDIENTS (SERVES 6–8):
450 g/1 lb boneless chicken, cubed
450 g/1 lb smoked sausage, diced
1 large onion, diced
1 small green pepper, diced
1 small red pepper, diced
6 cloves of garlic, minced
4 stalks celery, chopped
1 tube of tomato purée/paste
10 cups/2.4 litres/4 pints chicken stock/bouillon
1 x 400 g tin/can chopped tomatoes or 4 fresh tomatoes, chopped
3 tsp Creole Seasoning (readymade or see: Recipe No. 58)
2 tsp ground black pepper
2–4 tsp hot pepper sauce (to taste)
2 sprigs of fresh thyme
½–1½ tsp salt (to taste)
4 cups/800 g/28 oz long grain rice
450 g/1 lb shrimps/prawns (optional)

METHOD:

1. Brown the chicken and sausage in a heavy-bottomed pan.
2. Pour off all but 2 to 3 tablespoons of the fat. Set the meats aside in a covered dish.
3. In the frying pan, sauté the onion, green and red peppers, garlic and celery until the onion just starts to turn translucent.
4. Add the tomato purée/paste and cook over low heat for about 5 minutes. Add 2 cups of the chicken stock and stir until all the ingredients are well blended.
5. Add the tomatoes, Creole Seasoning, pepper, pepper sauce, thyme and salt to taste.
6. Cook over low-medium heat for about 10 minutes.
7. Add the meats and cook for another 7 minutes.
8. Add the rest of the stock/bouillon.
9. Stir in the rice, combining thoroughly.
10. Cover tightly.
11. Simmer for 20–25 minutes or until the rice is done.
12. If using, add the prawns/shrimps 7–10 minutes prior to the end of the cooking time.

No. 80 FRIED SPICY CHICKEN

Most likely to be found: All over the world.
Alternative Names: Southern Fried Chicken,
Caribbean Fried Chicken, Shake 'n' Bake Chicken.

THE SECRET: Seasoning chicken directly, rather than seasoning flour/breadcrumbs achieves the best tasting chicken. Also, do not over fry the chicken as this will make it dry and hard.

OTHER BACKGROUND INFORMATION: Healthier Option: Chicken can be baked in the oven for 40–45 minutes (instead of frying) which will produce similar results (but less greasy) provided that you have not removed the chicken skin prior to cooking.

INGREDIENTS (SERVES 4–6):
1 whole chicken or 8 chicken pieces – legs and thighs
3 tbsp vinegar (optional)
1 onion, finely chopped
2 tsp chopped thyme
4 cloves of garlic, crushed
2 tsp black pepper
2 tsp paprika
3 escallion stalks, finely chopped
2 tsp chicken seasoning (optional)
1 tbsp soya sauce
1 tbsp vegetable oil
2 eggs
6–8 tbsp plain flour or breadcrumbs
3 cups cooking oil (for deep frying)

METHOD:

1. Prepare the chicken using the vinegar (optional). (See: *Meat and Fish Preparation – Caribbean Style*, page 9.)
2. Remove the excess liquid.
3. With a sharp knife trim off any excess fat, skin or sinew.
4. Add the chicken pieces to a large bowl and season with the onion, thyme, garlic, black pepper, paprika, escallion, chicken seasoning, soya sauce and 1 tablespoon of vegetable oil.
5. Cover the bowl and leave to marinade for 4–6 hours (or preferably overnight) in a refrigerator.
6. Remove from the refrigerator. Add the eggs to the bowl with the chicken and stir well.
7. Put the flour or breadcrumbs into a bowl or a clean plastic bag.
8. Place the chicken in the bowl/plastic bag one piece at a time and coat with the flour/breadcrumbs.
9. Remove each chicken piece/portion from the bag/bowl and then repeat.
10. Put the cooking oil in a Dutch Pot/large thick-bottomed pan on a medium heat. **(NB:** If you place the bottom tip of a wooden spoon into the heated oil and bubbles form, the oil is ready for frying.)
11. Add the chicken pieces to the pot/pan of hot oil two at a time and fry for 5–7 minutes until golden brown.
12. Remove the cooked chicken from the hot oil and place on a rack/tray covered with kitchen paper/towels to remove excess oil.
13. Serve hot or cold.
14. Can be eaten with rice, potato, chips, salad.

No. 81 GUMBO (CREOLE)

Most likely to be found in: Louisiana.
Alternative Name: Creole Gumbo.

THE SECRET: Not burning the butter and making a smooth roux are the main secrets to a perfect Gumbo. Control of the cooking temperature is vital. Also you must keep stirring the roux at all times while it is cooking. DO NOT overcook the prawns/shrimps.

OTHER BACKGROUND INFORMATION: *Gumbo* is a stew that most probably originated in Louisiana during the eighteenth century. There are many different varieties of Gumbo. In New Orleans it is known as Creole Gumbo.

INGREDIENTS (SERVES 6):

5 cups/1.2 litres/2 pints chicken stock
1 white onion, chopped
4 escallion stalks, chopped
1 green pepper, chopped
1 tbsp Creole Seasoning
1 whole chicken, cut into portions (breasts, thighs, legs, etc.)
   or 8 chicken portions (thighs or breasts for best flavour)
3 tbsp butter
½ cup/75 g/2½ oz plain/all-purpose flour
2½ cups/600 ml/1 pint chicken stock
450 g/1 lb Creole smoked sausage, chopped

Optional Seafood:
1 cup prawns/shrimps
1 cup crawfish meat
1 cup crab meat

METHOD:

1. In a large heavy-bottomed pot, add the chicken stock, onion, escallions, pepper, Creole Seasoning and chicken portions.
2. Bring the pot to the boil and then reduce the heat and cook the chicken for approximately 35–45 minutes, until the meat is tender and no longer runs pink.
3. Drain off the liquid from the chicken, debone and then set to one side.
4. In a saucepan add the butter over medium heat and allow to melt until it goes nutty brown in colour (but not burnt).
5. Stir the flour into the melted butter to create a smooth dark brown roux.
6. Add the chicken stock, a small amount at a time, and whisk until the roux becomes a smooth dark brown sauce.
7. Add the boiled chicken pieces, sausage pieces and bring to the boil.
8. Cover the saucepan and simmer over the lowest heat for approximately 45 minutes.
9. If using, add the raw prawns/shrimps and other seafood to the pot and simmer for a further 8–10 minutes (until the prawns/shrimps are cooked).
10. Add salt and pepper to taste and then serve.

No. 82: CAJUN JAMBALAYA

Most likely to be found in: New Orleans.
Alternative Name: Red Jambalaya.

THE SECRET: For a good Cajun Jambalaya, the 'trinity of vegetables' should be in the proportion of 50 per cent onions, and 25 per cent each celery and green/red peppers. However, these proportions can be altered to suit your own individual taste.

OTHER BACKGROUND INFORMATION: Cajun Jambalaya unlike the Creole version does not contain any tomatoes.

INGREDIENTS (SERVES 6):
2 tsp olive oil
2 boneless skinless chicken breasts, cut into bite-size pieces
225 g/8 oz smoked sausage (kielbasa or andouille), diced
1 cup diced onion
½ cup diced green/red pepper
½ cup diced celery
2 tbsp chopped garlic
¼ tsp cayenne pepper
½ tsp onion powder
salt and ground black pepper (to taste)
2 cups/400 g/14 oz uncooked white long grain rice
4 cups/960 ml/32 fl oz chicken stock
3 bay leaves
2 tsp Worcestershire sauce
1 tsp hot pepper sauce

Optional Meat & Seafood:
1 cup shrimps/prawns
1 cup smoked ham, diced
1 cup crawfish
1 cup crab

METHOD:

1. Heat the oil in a large pot over medium high heat.
2. Sauté the chicken, diced sausage (and optional smoked ham) until lightly browned, about 5 minutes.
3. Stir in the onion, green/red pepper, celery and chopped garlic.
4. Season with the cayenne, onion powder, salt and pepper.
5. Cook for 5 minutes, or until the onion is tender and translucent.
6. Add the rice, and then stir in the chicken stock and bay leaves.
7. Bring to the boil, then reduce the heat. If using, add the shrimps/prawns, crawfish and/or crab meat. Stir, cover and simmer for 8–10 minutes, or until the rice is tender (ensuring that the shrimps/prawns are not overcooked).
8. Stir in the Worcestershire and hot pepper sauces.

No. 83 BANANA BREAD

Most likely to be found: All over the Caribbean.
Alternative Name: Banana Cake.

THE SECRET: This bread/cake should be light and moist.

OTHER BACKGROUND INFORMATION: The mixture will make 2 layer cake tins or approximately 18 cup cakes. The cup cakes should be baked at 350°F/180°C/Gas Mark 4 (160°C fan assisted oven) for 30 minutes.

INGREDIENTS (SERVES 6):
225 g/8 oz flour
2 tsp baking powder
¼ tsp nutmeg
100 g/4 oz butter or margarine
170 g/6 oz sugar
2 eggs, beaten
450 g/1 lb ripe bananas
1 tsp lime juice
1 cup/240 ml/8 fl oz milk

METHOD:
1. Sift the flour, baking powder and nutmeg together.
2. Cream the butter and sugar together.
3. Add the beaten eggs gradually to the creamed mixture.
4. Peel and mash or slice the bananas and add them to the mixture together with the lime juice.
5. Heat the oven to 350°F/180°C/Gas Mark 4 (160°C fan assisted oven).
6. Fold in the flour alternately with the milk. Put in a greased 8 inch/20 cm square tin.
7. Bake in the middle of the oven for around 1 hour.
8. To test whether the cake is done, insert a skewer or small knife into the centre of the cake and it should come out clean.

No. 84. GINGER CAKE

Most likely to be found: All over the Caribbean.

INGREDIENTS (SERVES 6):
225 g/8 oz butter or margarine
225 g/8 oz caster sugar
4 eggs
225 g/8 oz self-raising flour
50 g/2 oz mixed spice
2 tbsp ground ginger
50 g/2 oz ground almonds
2 tbsp milk

METHOD:
1. Cream together the butter or margarine and sugar until soft.
2. Lightly beat the eggs and gradually add to the butter/margarine mixture.
3. Sieve the flour, mixed spice and ground ginger together.
4. Mix with the ground almonds.
5. Stir gently into the butter or margarine with the milk until you get a smooth mixture.
6. Grease an 8 inch/20 cm cake tin.
7. Pour in the mixture.
8. Bake in the centre of a moderate oven 325°F/170°C/Gas Mark 3 (150°C fan assisted oven) for 1 hour or until done.
9. Leave to cool.

No. 85 COCONUT SWEET BREAD

Most likely to be found in: Barbados, Jamaica, Trinidad & Tobago
and most other islands of the Caribbean.
Alternative Name: Coconut Bread.

THE SECRET: The finished result should have a crunchy top with a
soft and moist cake below. Most of the Barbadian and Trinidadian recipes
use dried mixed fruit, but the Jamaican versions do not.

OTHER BACKGROUND INFORMATION: Every Caribbean
island has its own variation of this recipe which has been passed down
from generation to generation.

INGREDIENTS (SERVES 6):
170 g/6 oz butter or margarine
100 g/4 oz Demerara sugar
225 g/8 oz self-raising flour
200 g/7 oz plain flour
100 g/4 oz dried mixed fruit (optional)
100 g/4 oz desiccated (dried) coconut
5 ml/1 tbsp mixed spice
10 ml/2 tbsp vanilla essence
10 ml/2 tbsp rum
2 eggs, beaten
150 ml/¼ pint milk
caster sugar blended with ½ tsp water

METHOD:

NB: Soak desiccated coconut in milk for 30 minutes prior to use.

1. Preheat the oven to 350°F/180°C/Gas Mark 4 (160°C fan assisted oven).
2. Grease two 450 g/1 lb loaf tins.
3. Place the butter/margarine and sugar into a large mixing bowl and sift in all of the flour and mixed fruit.
4. Rub the ingredients together with your fingertips until the mixture resembles fine breadcrumbs.
5. Add the desiccated coconut, mixed spice, vanilla essence, rum, eggs and milk, and mix together.
6. If the mixture feels too dry then add more milk, if too wet then add more flour.
7. Turn out on a floured board and knead until firm and pliable.
8. Halve the mixture and place in each loaf tin. Glaze with sugared water.
9. Bake for 1 hour or until a skewer inserted into the loaf comes out clean.
10. Transfer to a wire/cake rack to cool. (Resist cutting it for 30 minutes or it might crumble.)

No. 86 BULLA CAKE

Most likely to be found in: Jamaica.
Alternative Names: Bullas, Bullah, Jamaican Bulla Cakes.

THE SECRET: Despite the name, bulla cakes tend to be heavier than most Caribbean cakes, and have a bun-like texture. Their colour should be beige to caramel brown.

OTHER BACKGROUND INFORMATION: Bulla Cake is often eaten with a sliced cheese (Bulla and Cheese) or sliced avocado filling (known as 'Bulla and Pear'). The colour of your bulla cakes depends greatly on the type of brown sugar used. The darker the sugar, the darker the colour, and vice versa.

INGREDIENTS (SERVES 8–10):
225 g/8 oz brown sugar
¼ tsp salt
2 cups/480 ml/16 fl oz water (sufficient water to create a
    heavy and clammy dough)
½ tsp ground ginger
2 tbsp butter/margarine, melted
3 tsp vanilla extract or 1 vanilla pod
3 cups/450 g/15 oz flour
1 tbsp baking soda
1 tsp ground cinnamon
¼ tsp ground nutmeg
½ tsp allspice

METHOD:

1. Preheat the oven to 350°F/180°C/Gas Mark 4 (160°C fan assisted oven).
2. In a saucepan dissolve the sugar, and salt in the water on low heat.
3. Add the ginger, butter/margarine and vanilla and stir until the ingredients have blended.
4. Remove the liquid from the heat and allow to cool (to touch, but not cold).
5. Sieve the flour, baking soda and ground spices into a mixing bowl.
6. Combine the cooled liquid with the dry ingredients in order to make the dough. The dough will be at the right consistency when it has a heavy and clammy texture.
7. Place the dough on a floured surface/board and dust with flour until the dough is manageable.
8. Roll out to a thickness of 0.75 cm and cut into 10–12.5 cm/ 4–5 inch diameter circles, using the rim of a large glass or cup.
9. Grease and lightly flour a baking tray/sheet.
10. With a floured spatula, place the bulla dough circles evenly on the tray/sheet.
11. Bake in the hot oven for 20–25 minutes.

No. 87 PUMPKIN PONE

Most likely to be found in: Guyana and other islands of the Caribbean.
Alternative Name: Pumpkin Pudding.

THE SECRET: Caribbean pones (pudding/sweetbreads) should have a crispy top and soft middle. This recipe is a Guyanese favourite which has made its way around the Caribbean and beyond.

OTHER BACKGROUND INFORMATION: You can also use this recipe to make Cassava Pone, by substituting the pumpkin for the same amount of grated Cassava.

INGREDIENTS (SERVES 6):
2 cups raw pumpkin
2 cups desiccated (dried) coconut or grated coconut
1 cup cornmeal flour
¼ cup brown sugar
3 tbsp butter/margarine
1 cup/240 ml/8 fl oz cold water
¼ tsp ground cinnamon
½ tsp grated nutmeg
1 tsp vanilla essence

METHOD:

1. Peel, wash and grate the pumpkin into a large bowl.
2. Add the desiccated coconut.
3. Add the cornmeal flour, sugar and butter/margarine.
4. Fold the water into the other ingredients until you have a creamy mixture.
5. Add the cinnamon, nutmeg and vanilla essence and continue to fold in.
6. Pour the mixture into a greased pan (or cupcake sheet/tart tins).
7. Bake at 350°F/180°C/Gas Mark 4 (160°C fan assisted) for 45 minutes to 1 hour until the pudding is cooked and golden brown on top.
8. Place aluminium foil over the top of the pudding (to prevent burning) if this part of the pudding is cooked before the rest.
9. Allow to cool and then cut into 5 cm/2 inch squares to serve.

No. 88 SPICED BUN

Most likely to be found in: Jamaica.
Alternative Names: Easter Bun, Easter Spiced Bun.

THE SECRET: The bun should be reasonably light and moist. Its unique flavour comes from the combination of ground cinnamon, ginger and nutmeg.

OTHER BACKGROUND INFORMATION: Spiced bun is a Jamaican favourite. *Bun 'n' Cheese* is a Jamaican favourite especially at Easter time. Jamaican processed cheeses can be found at specialist ethnic food stores or online (*Tastee* and *Sunjam* being the most widely available brands).

INGREDIENTS (SERVES 6):
1 standard bottle (340 ml/12 oz) dark stout (Dragon Stout or
    Guinness Stout)
1 cup/175 g/6 oz brown sugar
½ tbsp gravy browning
1 tbsp molasses/dark treacle
2 tbsp honey
2 tbsp butter
3 cups/450 g/15 oz plain/all-purpose flour
4 tsp baking powder
3 tsp ground cinnamon
1 tsp ground nutmeg
1 tsp ground ginger
1 cup mixed dried fruit
½ cup glazed cherries, diced

METHOD:

1. In a saucepan warm the stout on a low heat.
2. Add the brown sugar, gravy browning, molasses, honey and butter, and stir until the sugar has dissolved and the butter has melted.
3. Allow the mixture to cool down to room temperature.
4. Sieve the flour, baking powder and ground spices into a bowl.
5. Add the dried fruit and cherries.
6. Add the stout liquid mixture to the bowl and fold in the flour until you have a smooth mixture, which is difficult to stir. (**Alternatively**: use the dough hooks on a hand blender or food processor to obtain a lighter mixture.)
7. Preheat the oven to 275°F/140°C/Gas Mark 1 (120°C fan assisted) for about 12 minutes.
8. Pour the bun mixture into a greased bread/loaf tin/pans.
9. Bake in the cool oven for about 1–1½ hours.
10. Serve with processed cheese *('Bun 'n' Cheese)*.

No. 89 CARIBBEAN CHRISTMAS CAKE

Most likely to be found: All over the Caribbean.
Alternative Name: Black Cake.

THE SECRET: The longer you soak the fruit, the better the taste. Many people do not like fruit cake because of the big lumps of dried fruit. The secret of creating a fruit cake without any lumps of fruit is to use a food processor to blend the soaked fruit and alcohol into a fine purée.

OTHER BACKGROUND INFORMATION: Each island has its own special blend of dried fruit, fortified wines and rum, which gives its cakes a unique flavour. For an authentic Jamaican Christmas Cake *Wray & Nephew – Red Label Aperitif Wine* and a Jamaica Rum (*Appleton* or *Wray & Nephew*) should be used for soaking the fruit.

Trinidadian recipes tend to suggest that you soak the fruit/cake in a mixture of cherry brandy and a Trinidadian white rum such *Angostura*, *Puncheon* and *White Oak*.

Makes 3 or 4 cakes, depending on the size of the cake/baking tins.

INGREDIENTS (SERVES 12–16):
225 g/½ lb dark raisins★
225 g/½ lb golden raisins★
225 g/½ lb currants
450 g/1 lb dried/glazed cherries
225 g/½ lb mixed candied citrus peel
1 tsp grated nutmeg
2 cups dark rum; more for brushing cake
2 cups fortified/cooking wine (cherry brandy, sherry)
1½ cups rum
100 g/4 oz blanched almonds
450 g/1 lb butter; plus more for buttering pans
450 g/1 lb/about 2½ cups light or dark brown sugar
¼ cup browning (for colouring mixture) or 1 cup sugar and
    ½ cup water (for making your own browning)
10 eggs
zest of 2 limes/1 lemon
3 tsp vanilla extract

4 cups/450 g/16 oz plain/all–purpose flour
4 tsp baking powder
1 tsp ground cinnamon
¼ cup dark molasses or dark treacle (for colouring mixture)

Optional Ingredients:
225 g/½ lb prunes (with stones removed) *NB: If prunes are
used you should reduce the amount of raisins used to ¼ lb
of dark and ½ golden.
½ tbsp Angostura bitters

METHOD:
1. At least one week before baking, combine the raisins, currants,
cherries, candied peel, nutmeg and prunes (if using), and place in a
sealable jar or container.
2. Cover with a mixture of rum (light or dark) and your favourite
fortified/cooking wine (sherry).
3. Cover the jar tightly. Shake or stir occasionally.
4. When ready to bake, put the soaked fruit and almonds in a blender
or food processor; work in batches that the machine can handle.
5. Grind to a rough paste, leaving some chunks of fruit intact. Add a
little brandy or wine if needed to loosen the mixture in the machine.
6. Heat the oven to 275°F/140°C/Gas Mark 1. Butter three
22.5 cm/9-inch or four 20 cm/8-inch cake pans; line the bottoms
with a double layer of parchment or greaseproof/wax paper.
7. In a mixer, cream the butter with the light or dark brown sugar and
browning until smooth and fluffy. **NB:** You can make your own
browning by melting 1 cup of caramelized sugar until dark brown
and then adding water to the mixture. Or you can buy pre-made
browning in a bottle.
8. Mix in the eggs one at a time, then the lime zest, vanilla and bitters.
9. Transfer the mixture to a very large bowl. In a separate bowl,
combine the flour, baking powder and cinnamon.
10. Fold the dry ingredients into the butter mixture.
11. Stir in the fruit paste, browning (burnt sugar) and molasses. The
batter should be a medium-dark brown; if too light, add a tablespoon
or two of molasses or dark treacle.
12. Divide the batter among the prepared lined cake tins/pans.

13. Bake for 2–3½ hours at 275°F/140°C/Gas Mark 1, checking every 15 minutes after 2 hours; it may take 2–3 hours longer, until a skewer can be inserted into the centre of each cake and come out clean. (**NB**: Place silver foil on top of the cakes if they start to burn but aren't fully cooked.)
14. Remove the cakes to a rack. While the cakes are still warm, brush them with rum/wine mixture and let it soak in.
15. Repeat while the cakes cool; they will absorb about 4 tablespoons in total. When the cakes are completely cool, they can be turned out and served.
16. To keep longer, wrap the cakes tightly in greaseproof/wax or parchment paper, then in foil.
17. Store in a cool, dry place for up to 2 months.

No. 90 SWEET POTATO PUDDING

Most likely to be found in: Jamaica and the Caribbean.

THE SECRET: This pudding should have a hard crust and base, and soft, gooey middle. The colour is very much dependent on the type of brown sugar used.

OTHER BACKGROUND INFORMATION: In Jamaica traditionally this dish was cooked in a Dutch Pot in a coal pit with hot coals/wood underneath and on top.

INGREDIENTS (SERVES 6):
900 g/2 lb sweet potatoes
50 g/2 oz margarine
1 tsp cinnamon
1 tsp vanilla
1 tsp nutmeg
2 eggs
150 ml/¼ pint milk
100 g/4 oz brown sugar
50 g/2 oz mixed fruit
1 tsp lime juice
1 tsp grated lime rind

METHOD:
1. Scrub the sweet potatoes, peel and cut into cooking pieces.
2. Boil in slightly salted water until done. Drain off water.
3. While hot, mash well, blending in the margarine and spices.
4. Beat the eggs, add the milk and sugar and stir until the sugar dissolves.
5. Add the egg and sugar mixture to the mashed potatoes, and fold in.
6. Add the mixed fruit, lime juice and lime rind.
7. Pour the mixture into a greased tin.
8. Bake in the oven at medium temperature at 350°F/180°C/Gas Mark 4 for 45 minutes to 1 hour until the pudding is cooked and golden brown on top.

No. 91 TROPICAL FRUIT SALAD

Most likely to be found: All over the Caribbean.
Alternative Name: Caribbean Fruit Salad.

THE SECRET: A very simple recipe which can be varied to suit one's own tastes in exotic fruits.

OTHER BACKGROUND INFORMATION: Many Caribbean/ tropical exotic fruits are not available the whole year round (or if they are may be very expensive) so you may need to vary ingredients based on local availability.

INGREDIENTS (SERVES 6):
1 fresh pineapple
2 mangoes
1 honeydew melon
2 kiwi fruit
½ bunch of red grapes (or ½ punnet of strawberries)
½ bunch of green grapes
1 paw paw
1 litre carton of mango, orange or apple juice
450 g/1 lb ripe bananas

METHOD:
1. For all the fruit except the bananas: peel (if necessary), cut into small pieces and put into a bowl with the mango, orange or apple juice (or a combination of the three).
2. Slice the bananas just before you are ready to serve and add to the fruit salad.
3. Serve on its own or with cream or ice cream.

No. 92 PEANUT PUNCH

Most likely to be found: All over the Caribbean.

THE SECRET: A very simple recipe, to which special 'family' secret ingredients can be added (like *Irish Moss Drink*) to give it an individual taste.

OTHER BACKGROUND INFORMATION: Peanut Punch is a high protein, energy drink in the Caribbean. It is also regarded by many as an aphrodisiac.

INGREDIENTS (SERVES 6):
1 litre/2 pints milk (whole or semi-skimmed)
4 tbsp peanut butter
1 large tin/can (400 g approx.) or 2 x small tins/cans (200 g
    approx) condensed milk
¾ tsp nutmeg
¾ tsp cinnamon
1 tsp vanilla essence
1 cup/240 ml/8 fl oz rum (optional)
water (to taste)

METHOD:
1. Add the milk, peanut butter and condensed milk into a food processor and blend until smooth.
2. Add the nutmeg, cinnamon and vanilla essence.
3. For a stronger alcoholic flavour add one cup of rum (optional).
4. Taste. Dilute with water to taste (as necessary) if too sweet. Chill and serve.

No. 93 RUM PUNCH

Most likely to be found: All over the Caribbean.

THE SECRET: The secret to a good rum punch is finding the right balance between the taste of the rum and the taste of the other ingredients. Personal preference plays a big part in this recipe.

OTHER BACKGROUND INFORMATION: Why not try experimenting with different varieties of Caribbean rums, which are now widely available online or in specialist stores?

INGREDIENTS (SERVES 6):
1 cup white rum
1 cup dark rum (optional)
1 cup amber rum (optional)
1 cup coconut rum (optional)
8 fresh limes or 6 tbsp lime juice
2 cups grenadine or strawberry syrup
4 cups orange juice
4 dashes Angostura bitters (optional)
1 nutmeg, freshly grated (optional)
2 cups pineapple juice
ice cubes
water melon juice (optional)
1 orange, thinly sliced
water (to taste)

METHOD:
1. Mix all the ingredients together in a blender or punch bowl.
2. Sweeten to taste (or add extra fruit juice/water if too sweet).
3. Pour over ice cubes in any type of glass.
4. Dilute with water to taste (as necessary) if too sweet or too strong.

No. 94 CARROT JUICE

Most likely to be found: All over the Caribbean.
Alternative Name: Carrot Punch.

THE SECRET: Like most other Caribbean juices/punches the secret of great Carrot Juice is getting the right blend of the ingredients so that no single ingredient overpowers the others.

OTHER BACKGROUND INFORMATION: Carrot juice is said to have many health benefits.

INGREDIENTS (SERVES 6):
900 g/2 lb carrots, grated
1 litre/2 pints milk (whole or semi-skimmed)
1 large tin/can (400 g approx.) or 2 x small tins/cans
   (200 g approx.) condensed milk
¾ tsp nutmeg
¾ tsp cinnamon
1 tsp vanilla essence or 1 cup rum (optional)
water (to taste)

METHOD:
1. Wash the carrots and remove the tops and ends.
2. Grate the carrots with a vegetable grater or food processor.
3. Add the milk and condensed milk to the grated carrots and stir.
4. Use a food processor to blend the carrots and milk mixture until smooth.
5. Squeeze and strain off the liquid and discard the carrot pulp.
6. Add the nutmeg, cinnamon and vanilla essence. Or for adults, replace the vanilla essence with a cup of rum.
7. Taste.
8. Dilute with water to taste (as necessary) if too sweet.
9. Chill and serve.

No. 95 SORREL

(DRINK)

Most likely to be found: All over the Caribbean.
Alternative Name: Sorrell Drink.

THE SECRET: Dried sorrel sepals are now widely available in ethnic food stores and markets and on the internet.

OTHER BACKGROUND INFORMATION: Not to be confused with the vegetable of the same name from temperate countries. Sorrel is a favourite Caribbean Christmas and New Year drink. It is usually prepared in two batches (one with alcohol and the other without).

INGREDIENTS (SERVES 6):
2.5 cm/1 inch square piece of ginger
450 g/1 lb dry sorrel sepals
20 cups water
5 tbsp brown sugar
1 cup rum

Optional Spices:
1 tsp cloves
1 tsp ground pimenta (allspice)
1 tsp cinnamon
1 tbsp orange peel
1 tbsp lemon peel
1 tsp mace

Optional Alcohol:
1 cup wine
1 cup fortified wine
5 cups rum

METHOD:
1. Grate the ginger.
2. Add the ginger, sorrel and water to a pot and rapidly bring to the boil.
3. Add a selection of the Optional Spices to the mixture to personalise the drink.
4. Allow the mixture to boil for 10 minutes and then remove from the heat.
5. Once the mixture has cooled, place in a refrigerator for 24 hours.
6. Remove from the refrigerator and strain the mixture.
7. Stir in the sugar and 1 cup of rum (which will act as a preservative).
8. If desired add some or all of the Optional Alcohol at this stage.
9. Chill or serve with ice.

No. 96 GOLDEN APPLE DRINK

(NATIONAL DRINK: ST VINCENT)

Most likely to be found: All over the Caribbean.
Alternative Names: June Plum Wine, Ambarella Wine.

THE SECRET: The secret to this recipe is naturally the Caribbean June Plum or Golden Apple (*Spondias dulcis*). This fruit is widely available on most Caribbean islands and in Asia, but is more difficult to find in other areas of the world.

OTHER BACKGROUND INFORMATION: This fruit has many different names including: Golden Apple (St Vincent, St Lucia), June Plum (Jamaica), Pomcite (Trinidad & Tobago), Jobo, Malay Apple, Dew Plum and Pomme Cyth're, Ambarella, Prune de Cythre and Spondias dulcis. For a picture of this fruit go to www.tntisland.com/fruits.html and see: 'June Plum'.

INGREDIENTS (SERVES 6):
12 large ripe June Plums (Golden Apples)
4 tsp nutmeg
sugar (to taste)
½ tsp vanilla essence
2.3 litres/4 pints hot water
2 cups white/dark rum (optional)

METHOD:

1. Wash and peel the June Plums (Golden Apples).
2. Remove the apple cores, and then cut or grate the apples to remove the flesh and chop.
3. Put the apple peel, pulp (excluding seeds) in a jar.
4. Add the nutmeg, sugar (to taste), vanilla essence, hot water and rum.
5. Stir the mixture until most of the sugar has dissolved.
6. Cover and leave the mixture for 48 hours in a cool, dark place to allow for mixture to ferment.
7. Strain the mixture and discard the pulp, and store in the refrigerator.
8. Serve over ice.

No. 97 GUINNESS PUNCH

Most likely to be found in: Jamaica, Trinidad
and other Caribbean Islands.
Alternative Name: Guinness Stout Punch.

THE SECRET: *Guinness® Stout* (as opposed to the more widely available *Guinness Original* or *Guinness Draught*) is the key ingredient in this popular Caribbean drink. Optional ingredients such as vanilla essence, Caribbean flavours mixed essence, unsweetened cocoa powder and rum will all make this drink more exotic.

OTHER BACKGROUND INFORMATION: *Guinness Punch* is very popular and in some ways similar to Irish Moss. It was introduced to the Caribbean by the Irish, and is believed to boost energy and give an increased libido.

This recipe isn't suitable for those who are advised not to consume raw eggs, such as pregnant women or the elderly.

INGREDIENTS (SERVES 6):
6 x 12 oz/330 ml bottles Guinness Stout
½ cup/120 ml/4 fl oz sweetened condensed milk
2 eggs (raw and beaten – optional)
¾ tsp cinnamon
¾ tsp nutmeg
¾ tsp unsweetened cocoa powder (optional)
½ tsp vanilla essence (optional)
½ tsp Caribbean Flavours Mixed Essence (optional)
1 cup white rum (optional)

METHOD:
1. Add the Guinness Stout, condensed milk and egg to a blender. Mix the ingredients.
2. Pour the drink into a covered drink jug. Add the cinnamon and nutmeg, and then stir.
3. Add the other optional ingredients to your taste.
4. Place the punch in the refrigerator to chill. Serve cold.

No. 98 SOURSOP PUNCH/JUICE

Most likely to be found: All over the Caribbean.
Alternative Name: Guanabana Punch.

THE SECRET: Fresh soursop/guanabana fruit is the key to this drink, but is very hard to find.

OTHER BACKGROUND INFORMATION: In the US fresh soursop/guanabana fruit can be ordered online (in season) directly from specialist fruit growers. In the UK you may be able to find frozen, canned and/or puréed versions in your local ethnic food store or market. Ethnic food stores also often stock the canned fruit or carton juices under the name Guanabana.

INGREDIENTS (SERVES 6):
1 ripe large sized soursop/guanabana, peeled, deseeded and
  sliced
1 cup milk
5 tbsp sugar (add more or less to taste)
1 cup crushed ice
1 squeezed lime (optional)
1 cup water (optional)

METHOD:
1. Blend the soursop, milk and sugar in a food processor.
2. Add the ice and optional lime juice, and blend again until smooth.
3. Add more sugar and water if necessary (to taste).

No. 99 CARIBBEAN FRUIT PUNCH

Most likely to be found: All over the Caribbean.

THE SECRET: Like most other Caribbean juices/punches/juice drinks the secret is getting the right blend of the ingredients so that no single ingredient overpowers the others.

OTHER BACKGROUND INFORMATION: Try to create your own fruit punch by experimenting with the variety of exotic fruit juices now widely available in local supermarkets and convenience stores including: *Mango, Passion fruit, Pineapple, Lychee, Guava, Guanabana, Pomegranate, Papaya* and *Watermelon* (to name but a few).

INGREDIENTS (SERVES 15):
1 litre orange juice
1 litre pineapple juice
1 litre mango juice
1 litre of any other exotic fruit juice of your choice (optional)
1 cup lime/lemon juice (optional)
1 cup strawberry syrup (grenadine syrup)
2 cups rum (optional)
1 x tin/can fruit salad (optional)
water (to taste)

METHOD:
1. Mix all the ingredients together in a bowl.
2. Taste, and dilute with water if too sweet.
3. Allow to chill and then serve over ice or with pieces of fruit salad.

No. 100 PINEAPPLE PUNCH

Most likely to be found: All over the Caribbean.

THE SECRET: This punch has a tendency to be too sweet, so to avoid this you may need to dilute with water or milk, to taste. Also the dominant taste should be pineapple so on final tasting add some more pineapple juice if this key ingredient has been overpowered by the other ingredients.

INGREDIENTS (SERVES 6):
1 litre/1¾ pints pineapple juice
½ cup/120 ml/4 fl oz sweetened condensed milk
¼ tsp cinnamon
¼ tsp nutmeg
½ tsp vanilla essence (optional)
½ tsp Caribbean Flavours Mixed Essence (optional)
water/milk (to taste)

METHOD:
1. Add the pineapple juice, condensed milk, cinnamon and nutmeg to a blender.
2. Mix the ingredients.
3. Pour the drink into a covered drink jug.
4. Add the other optional ingredients to your taste.
5. Taste. Dilute with water or milk, as necessary, if the punch is too sweet.
6. Place the punch in the refrigerator to chill.
7. Serve chilled or over ice.

ABOUT US

David Daley

David grew up in Coventry, West Midlands working in *Gwen's Catering*, his mother Gwendolyn's catering business, with his late father Lyndon and his siblings. David's passion for Caribbean food and culture has been inspired by his parents' cooking and frequent visits to the Caribbean to see family and friends. David is the proprietor of **Roti Kitchen**, Caribbean Caterers specializing in events and outside catering (*www.rotikitchen.com* and *www.facebook.com/rotikitchen*).

Gwendolyn Daley

Gwen was born in Mandeville, Jamaica and was first noticed for her culinary excellence at the age of 12 when she won a baking competition at her local school. This earned her a scholarship (specialising in cookery) for a college in Montego Bay. Gwen moved to the UK in the early 1960s and settled in the West Midlands. With the help of her family Gwen ran her own Caribbean catering company for over 40 years. Gwen is now retired, but continues to run a cookery club for adults and children in her local community and helped her son, David establish his own catering business.

WHERE TO FIND CARIBBEAN FOOD INGREDIENTS ONLINE

IN THE UK
- Afro Caribbean Store (Southampton): www.afrocaribbeanstore.co.uk
- AfroCarib UK (Essex): www.afrocarib.co.uk
- Avila UK (London): www.avilauk.com
- Baron Foods UK (London): www.baronfoods.com
- Bluenet Foods (Wolverhampton): www.bluenetfoods.co.uk
- Caribbean Supermarket: www.caribbeansupermarket.co.uk
- Caribbean Trade UK Ltd (Coventry): www.caribbeantrade.co.uk
- E & J Brand UK (London): www.eandjbrands.co.uk
- Grace Food UK (Welwyn Garden City): www.gracefoods.co.uk and www.caribbeanfoodcentre.com
- My Afro Foodstone (Dartford, Kent): www.myafrofoodstore.com
- Tee's Caribbean Recipe Kits (London): www.caribbeanrecipekits.com
- The Asian Cookshop – Caribbean Food Online: www.theasiancookshop.co.uk/caribbean-food-online-59-c.asp
- Tropical Sun Foods (London): www.tropicalsunfoods.com (products are available via amazon.co.uk)

Caribbean Food Brands available in the UK
- Chief (Trinidad & Tobago): www.chief-brand.com
- Dunn's River Foods: See: Grace Foods Groups
- Encona Sauces (Grace Foods Group): www.enconasauces.co.uk
- Grace Foods Group, Welwyn Garden City: www.gracefoods.com and www.gracefoods.co.uk
- Juliana's Authentic Jamaican & Nel's Old Time: www.tijulecompany.com
- Linstead Market (Jamaica): www.linsteadmarketja.com
- P A Benjamin Manufacturing Co Ltd: www.pabenjamin.com

- Royal Caribbean Bakery (New York): www.royalcaribbeanbakery.com
- Tropical Sun Foods: www.tropicalsunfoods.com
- Walkerwood Caribbean Food: www.walkerswood.com

IN THE USA
- First World Imports: www.firstworldimports.com/store
- Grace Foods USA: www.gracefoods.com
- Island Boy Trading Wholesale Distributor: www.islandboytrading.com
- Sam's Caribbean Superstore (New York): www.sams247.com

ACKNOWLEDGEMENTS

Firstly we must thank our editor Judith Mitchell for her patience and understanding, and Martin Palmer for his encouragement and support.

We would also like to thank our family and friends who have supported us in the writing of this cookbook as well as the chefs we have worked with who have shared their recipes, tips and secrets over the years.

INDEX